PTOLEMY'S DISCIPLE

Gottfried Benn

PTOLEMY'S DISCIPLE

Edited, Translated and with a Preface by
SIMONA DRAGHICI, PhD

PLUTARCH PRESS
CORVALLIS, OR

For information, address the publisher:
PLUTARCH PRESS
P.O. Box 195, Corvallis, OR 97339-0195, USA

Library of Congress Cataloging-in-Publication Data

Benn, Gottfried, 1886-1956.
   [Ptolemäer. English]
   Ptolemy's disciple / Gottfried Benn ; edited, translated and with a preface by Simona Draghici.
     p. cm.
   Contents: Ptolemy's disciple -- The radar thinker.
   ISBN 0-943045-20-7 (pbk. : alk. paper)
    I. Benn, Gottfried, 1886-1956. Radar Denker. English. II. Draghici, Simona, 1937- III.
Title: Radar thinker. IV. Title.

PT2603.E46P713 2005
834'.912--dc22

           2005042974

Manufactured in the United States of America.
Book design and cover by JAY.

CONTENTS

PREFACE

These are the first two important prose works that Gottfried Benn wrote after the war with Germany came to an end in the Spring of 1945 — the Soviet Army conquered the street on which he lived in Berlin on the very day Hitler committed suicide: 30 April 1945. Benn began making notes for PTOLEMY'S DISCIPLE as early as February 1946, and the three chapters of the Berlin novella were completed between April and September 1947: the first in April, the second in August, and the third in September of the same year. There are no particular notebooks for THE RADAR THINKER, but the very fact that it took Benn less than three months (between early August and late October 1949) to complete it makes one presume that its gestation ran parallel with that of the novella, and to an extent, it may be considered an appendage to it, an epistemological coda: the occupied Berlin as the main stage is still there, only the hairdresser is replaced by the old physician with plenty of free time on his hands, who spends his idle moments looking out of his window from where more vistas open to him. PTOLEMY'S DISCIPLE is a novella only to the extent it is a collection of local events, prosaic, political, amorous, rendered in a satirical or humorous vein, and its lack of narrative and well-defined characters makes it a closer relation to the informal essay, which THE RADAR THINKER is, hence both the stylistic and the editorial compatibility of the two, as well.

They preceded his elaboration of the panoramic montage that was published under the title DOUBLE LIFE: TWO SELF -REPRESENTATIONS, in March 1950 and in which fragments from them are easily recognizable. Nevertheless, between them he also managed to round off a dialogue (Gespräche) in Plato's manner, in December 1948. Called THREE OLD MEN, its source of inspiration were the contents of various discussions in the press, as well as occasioned by visits paid to him by returnees, foreigners, and other characters, discussions about the evolution of events, the stance assumed by various intellectuals in the first half of the 20th century, and about the incumbent future.

*Ultimately, PTOLEMY'S DISCIPLE was published in Feb-
ruary 1949 in book form together with a 1944 work, THE
NOVEL OF THE PHENOTYPE, and an even earlier piece,
WOLF'S TAVERN, the arduous fruit of Benn's stay away from
Berlin, in Hannover with the Army, most of it as a probation-
er for the position of staff surgeon with the rank of major.
Benn had tinkered at it for two years between 1936 and 1938,
ever unsatisfied with the result. That collection was the first
publication in Germany of any ampler work by him since 1936.
On the other hand, he was dissuaded by his wife and friend
Oelze from presenting THE RADAR THINKER for publication,
with the result that it was first printed only posthumously, in
1958, in Volume II of THE COLLECTED WORKS IN FOUR
VOLUMES, edited by Dieter Wellershoff. Benn, however, had
not let it go to waste, but as it had been his habit, used
snipets of it in his 'radio-play' THE VOICE BEHIND THE
SCREEN (March 1952). Not unlike some composers, and fewer
poets, he had no qualms about recycling themes, phrases,
sentences, ideas, as he went along composing his 'little things'.
Thus, for instance, the first five maxims of the glass-blower
had first been articulated in a letter to his friend Oelze in
1936!*

*Nevertheless, unlike some of his critics, Benn evolved as
time went by, and that was in part due to his unusual sensitiv-
ity to what it was in the air, so to speak, and given the
ambiguity of human expression, some of his stylistic formulae
were made to convey different states of mind in keeping with
the change in the surroundings. Thus what had been Rönne's
day-dreaming continued to be a 'breathing space', but it was
no longer a substitute for the weakening capacity of individual
self-fulfilment in middle life, but a sociological filling of the
inner void, the result of so much dust from the ruined world
about him that had ultimately collapsed in more than one way.*

*Accordingly, Benn's creative activity may be divided into
three periods: the first, approximately between 1910 and
1920; the second, between 1920 and 1936, and the third, between 1936 and 1956, yet throughout his creative life, he
remained a poet, and this is very important to remember when
confronted with his prose, in particular. It is the prose of a
poet, in which narration assumes the form of stage directions
in a play, and the characters are increasingly reduced to a few
strokes descriptive of the outside appearance, to become*

simply opportunities for the author to air his views about the confusion and the haphazards of life fully controlled by chance, life that could be led by a perpetual improvisation, and which makes the maxim 'discern the situation' on each and every occasion the imperative for survival, in all the acceptations of the term. Like Goethe, one of his role models, Benn was self-centred ('all revolves round all, and when everything turns round everything, nothing turns but round itself' - p. 4), and devoid of that kind of imagination needed to concoct plots and characters, develop and direct them through the evolution. Most of the incidents and the scenery in his works were drawn from life, either from direct experience or from readings as well as from his contemplation of works of fine art during his frequent visits to museums and galleries, or in reproductions; magazines and newspapers were his richest source of information, and by the way, quite often his ampler informal essays, as a result, recall the layout of a journal. His were the three voices to which T.S. Eliot refers in his lecture 'The Three Voices of Poetry' (November 1953): Benn talks to himself (the diary style); he addresses one or another of his intimates (the letter style), and he also uses the indirect address by devising very summary characters, actually pegs on which he hangs his own ideas and experiences, as the patron fleeced by his daughter (p.9), or the 'gentleman from Ascot' (pp.20–22), or 'Infinity' (p.4). In Benn's case, the three media intertwine, and it is this, together with the juxtaposition of opposites, that lends thrust or propulsive force to his prose writings, the tension that awakens the feeling of immediacy in the reader. The diary, the letter, the dialogue, the journal and the stage directions are forms of expression, that once fragmented, are re-assembled into a coherent whole. not unlike a jigsaw puzzle. The critical distance which made Benn note down what he saw is concomitant with the need to assemble the reality by bundling the observations about the world in a perspective. It is in this especially that Benn's prose differs from Goethe's. Benn got more economical with his words as time went by, he did not tamper with them as Joyce did in his FINNEGANS WAKE, but concentrated on the pithiness of the phrase and after 1936, preferred the aphorism as the most appropriate form of expression in the climate of opinion of a genocidal world, and cared little for the number of pages he would cover, whereas Goethe used fillers extensively to pad his manuscripts,

viii

regardless of coherence and the effect on his readers. In Benn's case, the aphorism had also a technical function, namely to stimulate the author's train of thought, acting as a provocation. Furthermore, the pre-eminent poet, Goethe resorted to another device, from the non-human sphere, to construct the plot of his last novel in prose, ELECTIVE AFFINITIES (1809), namely, the principle of the affinity of chemical elements that is the attractive force between particles or substances, which makes them enter and remain in chemical combinations. Benn too, living in the full age of technology, made use of the principle of radar, taken from physics and referring to the electronic system that detects objects hidden by distance, darkness or clouds by means of radio waves, and to the related concepts of echo and reflection, as the axle on which the actors in THE RADAR THINKER gyrate and ratiocinate; yet, his approach is different: he did not impose a borrowed outline on his characters, but started from them as the source of the contemplative act, his direction is outwards. What Benn had been finding out on his own was that many of the discoveries and theories in such fields as astronomy, cybernetics and radiophysics are quite often confirmations of long-held human intuitions, or reformulations of old intuitions by different means.

*

Gottfried Benn's third creative period is perhaps the most relevant to us, unless we persist in misrepresenting his work blindly in order to indulge our self-sufficiency. It coincides with the transition from the bourgeois liberal democracy of a Second Reich to dictatorship, proletarian, populist or totalitarian, a truly world war, genocide and pastoralization, and continuous latent war. If the first period was characterized by the poet's confrontation with the realities of Wilhelminian Germany, and of the profession he had chosen for himself, the second had to do with the salvaging not only of the dignity of a humiliated nation, but of its very physical existence in the conditions of massive transfer and destruction of wealth, while the third period expanded beyond the confines of nation and continent to embrace the entire world. He no longer attempted to bring together north and south, but went on to contemplate the intercourse of the Western civilization with the rest of the planet, throughout history, which he tried to catch in the network of the word and then release once more in the *relativity of the universe. It enabled Benn, never an adept of synthesis, to indulge his mastery of non–Hegelian dialectics, to juggle with opposites, at times only by implication, from which the pathos, mistaken for sentimentalism, of the first period has disappeared for good, giving way to irony and cynicism, the latter acquiring a positive value in circumstances of mindless genocide. If basically irony implies a contradiction between the apparent and the real, or between what is and what ought to have been, cynicism, on the other hand, is not situational but only personal, given that it refers to the conduct of people that has been found wanting, to disappointed expectations which in turn breed distrust and contempt for those held guilty of inconsistency. In practical life, it may become a licence for extreme action in the guise of redress or justice, but that is not Benn's case: at most, his cynicism gives way to fury and indignation, and most often to sarcasm. Whatever may be said to the contrary, Benn had always been a moralist. His greatest disappointment was the human inability to learn from experience, and to change under the impact of extreme adversity ('a certain consensus has been reached as far as shades of cinnamon, ginger and amber for shawls and handbags in this low season,... and the rouge baiser and After Shave lotion are once more available in adequate quantities amidst the ruins.'– p.32). The absolute relativity of opportunism makes of the individual an end in himself, and it is against this background that Benn tried to outline a morality for the creative individual, and as another Cassandra, ended THE RADAR THINKER on a visionary note, granting humanity a new lease on life, this time on its own, but not too soon and not too easily. Gottfried Benn's irony has the cathartic effect that makes living in adversity bearable, as it allows the individual that inner space necessary for his awareness to grow more aware of the real dimensions of his situation. The core concepts, also appearing in the titles of both works, in their turn imply the presence of two different scales of values: one, distal, and the other, proximal; the absence of any one from the reader's awareness is likely to lead him into the pitfall of literalism and make him join those who have openly labelled him by turns a pig (the SS), a cretin (the communists), an intellectual prostitute (the democrats), a renegade (the emigrants), or a pathologic nihilist (the religious). They are 'core concepts' and not merely metaphors because they are not simple comparisons between two objects, as one is identified with the other. Thus, by 'Ptolemy's disciple', Benn wanted to convey his adherence to a world view that he found more adequate to the human dimension, that does not crush man under a time and space measured in billions of units, reducing him to a trace, at the very best. He explained it himself in a letter of 17 April 1947 to Fritz Werner, a Freiburg bookseller and bibliographer:'Ptolemy was the founder of the pre-Galilean world representation – the Earth is a disk encircled by Okeanos and bounded by the Pillars of Hercules. All stood still, lying shut in, making itself accessible to the human glance and thought. Then the cataclysm started.... To be sure, I do not believe in modern physics, it is part of the post-antiquity* **dynamic** *world image: of which the West is so proud...'. On the other hand, it is the self-absorbtion of the self-centred man that amasses and carries in him his universe, which in the case of the creative individual (the glass-blower) is the mass that softened by the heat of gestation and artistic inspiration, is blown into, by means of a hollow pipe, inflated to a bubble, and shaped into a vessel that is ultimately cut off the pipe by a stroke from the glass-blower, when he decides that he has achieved the desired result. He is the opposite of the 'radar man' who lacks both the substance and the creative urge, as he acts by reflection alone, mirroring light or other radiations, self-centred but incapable of any introspection and of any thought whatsoever concerning the essentials of being or even the daily existence. On the other hand, borrowed from THE ODYSSEY, Book IX, 90-104, the concept of lotus-eater and implicitly of the lotus-land is used to convey the craving for illusions, in forms as much as outside time, the longing for a place where one can hope and forget and all one's needs are satisfied by eating a miraculous fruit, that of the lotus: 'yet analyzed but still free were only the dreams. But all that was possible because the inner life, which I obviated in that way, found a substitute as soon as the self was blissfully evaded' (p. 7). To that notion Benn added the aesthetic aspect of the oriental lotus, the purity of which contrasts with the stagnant, muddy waters from which it issues, symbol also of prosperity and of the primordial matter, only to realize that everywhere it was an ephemeral self-deception and its ritual, a mechanical performance from which any sense of the unity of being was absent: 'the jewel in the lotus' seemed now more appropriate* as the trade name for a cosmetic product, a telling instance of the Bennlike irony. Nevertheless, through modern technology, symbolized here by Fermi's controlled nuclear chain reaction, cybernetics, genetics or the radar system, alongside of such age-old human propensities as that implicit in the principle of the Japanese garden, the human brain opens unsuspected and unpredictable vistas for human development, in the void created by millenia of introversion ('now begins the first ligature of Act II' - p.56), but it is the artist on whom ultimately devolves the main role in the delivery, as the only agent who can give expression to and serve jointly the spiritual and the material in man ('The artist is the only one who will get through the things and will decide on them' - p.24).

Some years ago I wrote somewhere else, that like William Butler Yeats, Gottfried Benn was not an original thinker; he himself admitted it: 'I am sure that the above mentioned facts have long been known to mature people..., they will find them banal, but I had to go through my overviews slowly' (p.27). Benn's originality, like Yeats', resides in the way he selects from, reformulates and presents his material, accummulated from a universe from which time and distance are banished, and where only the substance and the moment count.

Simona Draghici

EDITOR'S NOTE

Until now I have used the word 'Ptolemean' whenever I have been referring to Benn's work, unaware that it was a malapropism, and that the correct English word for an adept of Ptolemy's system is 'Ptolemaist' (and the derivative adjective is 'Ptolemaic'). My rather belated discovery requires that some rectifications be carried out. However, because I find the correct English word clumsy and remote, I have used it only once, in the text, preferring a paraphrase for the titles.

The Wellershoff edition, listed in the Short Bibliography at the end of this book, has been used for the translations, but the latter have been collated with the German texts from the most recent edition of Benn's complete works, also known as the Stuttgart edition. In this latter edition, I have noticed that as far as the novella was concerned, the dashes, whether singly or in pairs, were preceded, or followed, by other punctuation marks, such as commas, colons and semicolons. That was not the case of THE RADAR THINKER, where the dashes were kept free of other marks. However unusual that may seem in an English translation, Benn's idiosyncratic punctuation has been adhered to, though in the case of too long and convoluted periods, I did not hesitate to divide them into shorter sentences, while preserving the rhythm of the whole, and the dashes. Punctuation has a special importance in Benn's works, it is the equivalent of the composers' musical notations.

Another of Benn's idiosyncracies was to scatter foreign words and phrases over his texts as atmospherics, and also when he needed additional stresses in his descriptions. They have been left untranslated, but the sought-after effect is lost in the case of the English words, for which Benn, though claiming ignorance of the English language, seems to have had a particular weakness.

Some explanatory notes have been provided, placed as they are, at the back of the book. No attempt has been made to explain the countless allusions, classical or otherwise, in the texts. To produce a reader's digest has not been my intention as editor, and would not be a defensible enterprise.

PTOLEMY'S DISCIPLE
A BERLIN NOVELLA, 1947

I. LOTUS LAND

A horrible winter is approaching its end, with ups and downs from an ever renewed high pressure, which usually would make way for a so-called bright spell (obviously quite an extraordinary form on the scale of brightness). A truly malignant winter to which offerings of rudiments of furniture, baby cradles, broken pieces of debris were vainly made, a winter, which for four long months of -20°C, flayed the skin meant to protect the living.

Wolves on the Oder, vultures in the Müggelberge! A winter under the occupation! The municipal authorities entrench themselves behind the Occupation Powers, these, behind the elements, they in turn, probably behind the high plateau of Tibet, which immures itself behind some Dalai Lama, and so on and so forth -, in the mean time, everything goes to rack and ruin, businesses have gone to sleep, money has disappeared, taxes are no longer paid, life stalls. My business, a beauty salon, inclusive of varicose veins, has long succumbed. The treatment room had no heat for weeks. An arm out of the furcoat or a foot out of the rags would have meant a new pathology for the patrons. I was happy. No more frozen trotters and swollen fingers, itching bellies and varicose veins back and front! Finally, alone! Lastly, whenever the bell or the knocks at the door still annoyed me, I would point a machine-gun, which despite all the searches, I had recovered from the great struggle between peoples, and hidden in the adjacent street, and shoot all the suspects. The corpses did not look much different from those frozen to death and those who had dispatched themselves, they were lying on the pavement and the passers-by found that natural, - toothaches, an inflamed pulp might have made them react, but bulges in the snow -, they might be rats or bolsters.

Raskolnikov had killed an old pawnbroker and was tormented by it, he longed for atonement and forgiveness, - one of the most profound books of the white race described it incomparably, three quarters of a century ago -, today, the moral valuation of the so-called normal, but also of induced deaths was totally out of place, as was pleuresy or parricide;

only in the so-called administration of justice, especially in the staged monster trials, would one be reminded of the existence of juridical stipulations for the last blink and the last sigh. – If once upon a time, a certain moral fluid was running through man – and the reading of old scriptures makes us assume it as a probability – nowadays it has been fully put to rest. In a world, in which such monstruosities happen, a world that rests on such monstruous principles, which the new research presents as an established fact, it does not matter whether some people live several days longer or sleep a few more nights, one puts an end, at last, to this confusing chatter about life and happiness. Indeed, that is not the question. Matter was radiation and the divinity was silent, what lay in between was trivial. The creatures of the other world, just paper tigers, and the space between heaven and earth as hollow as a flute, but the Great Wall stands, and the loess has survived the Mings: – that, it seems to me, points to the pre-eminence of the amorphous.

And to proceed with the moral: I did not suffer in any form. The winter was too harsh, it hunted us down, it called for crimes. When sleeping at night, my breath would freeze over me and lay like a moskito net on my head, and when I turned, the skin on my face would chafe from this ice griddle, and wake me up. I would wake up from clear dreams. Infinity spoke to me, and it spoke thus:

'You think that Kepler or Galilei were the great beacons –, they were just loudmouthed old aunts. That the Earth revolves round the Sun was their knitted sock. Indeed, wholly fidgety, extrovert types. And now pay attention to the shrinking of this hypothesis! Today, all revolves round all, and when everything turns round everything, nothing turns but round itself. Of course it might be pointed out to the public, the "Rectification of Names," for instance, is a Chinese fundamental concept that to a certain extent is right, mankind evolves by means of propaganda –, but you are not advanced enough to be able to grasp it.'

Hyperborean nights! Another time I heard it talking like this:

'Take, for instance, the classical, also called the founding era of mathematics! The Descartes-Pascal-Leibnitz line – from 1630 until 1750 – tied to the splendid commentary on Euclid by Proclus, – and handed to us in the symbolic logic of Boole

4

and Peirce, of Russell and Hilbert --: aberrations, busyness, oddities! Small circle! During the same years, bigger circles strolled untroubled in the afternoon on the banks of the Nile or the Neva -, there the tasselled sashes of the Ethiopians, here the sports jacket; - coffee was gaining ground; Tinto in Brazil, Chico in Mexico, in the realm of the Mayas, on the ruins of the ancient Aztecs, - small talk under the primeval giant trees. But it goes even farther: residential estates, climate changes, storm damages, and also burnt theatres, genocides, usurpers -:where in all the world do reductions, extrema principles and field theories really make themselves mandatory and of identical value? One does not peep out beyond the familiar, cosy, small circle.'

As an island from the silt, those extraordinary observations of the night rose inside me and brightened my icy days. I was no enemy of mankind, although I must admit that on the telephone I would often ask those who wanted to see me, but please be punctual and do not stay too long. That, however, was out of a desire to observe certain formalities, and I owed it to myself. Too often I happened to face rotten eggs, husks: a certain European shrewdness, some genital erotica, and quite a few enterprising ideas about the State -, worn-out figures of speech, frayed counterarguments, and one sat through it all none the wiser -, but now the precepts from those bizarre dreams are in any case worth pondering on.

They certainly came close to my own line of observations. Intellectual life was hopeless, humanity without a core, perhaps still extant in beehives, substance relativized -, well, one caught it with one's hands, that was already popular. The prehistorical research has not racked its brains so hard and disinterested since 1900. The primitives too had their notion of energy, perceived connections, had a world of their own. They had knowledge, felt the magic effects of objects, they saw the unity and kept it up in the shudder of identity. In primitive cultures, space operated conditionally: what stood one next to the other was well-founded; at a later stage of their awareness, time happened; what occurred one after the other was grasped accordingly. Causality and the pocket watch - it was, I believe, associated with the name of Hume, but the glass and watch industries and the modern scientific world view - that was a new topic, and a truly unfathomable one. The scientific world view enunciated the propositions, then the scientific world view tested them, and afterwards, the scientific world view confirmed them (itself) and released them to the Press. It seemed to me somewhat disingenuous, although understandable. But, one would say, the comet still appears, and the solar eclipse still occurs, wholly motorized expeditions still travel to Brazil and similar coffee lands -, now, what happened down there, I had no idea; to my thinking, the telescopes made their appearance, and lenses and the index of refraction were turned round about, and whoever wanted to understand what was behind the comet and the solar eclipse, without them -, would hold a piece of blackened glass before his eyes and see the moon pass over the sun, as we used to do as children, and that seemed to me a fully satisfactory astronomy. For a long time these blown-up numbers and spaces, they too annoyed me, a businessman. The universe (according to Professor U of K University) disperses in all directions at a terrific speed, every single second, it spreads in all directions thirty-three times the diameter of the Earth: when, in my salon, something runs out of a perfume bottle or from a flask of toilet water, I can assess the whole damage with a blink. The universe (according to Professor K of U University) is ten billion years old, it is not to be assumed that it is considerably older -: my salon, even during the high season, is open only eight hours a day, so from the start, in the light of these ten billions, my situation is nothing to talk about. The universe (according to Professor X of U) 'already' draws its entire energy from the atomic transformation of hydrogen into helium -: well, now, as a specialist, I am familiar with hydrogen peroxide to bleach the hair, but this 'already' lives on a split. The only science, criticism, says that time and space are forms of our outlook, the world has got no time, and I hold this to be most likely; but now comes the other science, establishes this fragmentary time as historically extant and feeds on it with the help of these grotesque numbers. Something is not right there -, either - or; of course today's man demands from his newspaper the miracle of creation at regular intervals, but what they show here is a stagger cut -: were I to give my patrons such a haircut, none could go courting any longer.

Layman's attitude - certainly. Although I must admit, I have always had a weakness for speculative writings, fictions, combinations, deductive digressions, studied this and that, found Existentialism entertaining and read the literature on

6

categories as if it were a thriller by Edgar Wallace –, with me, a special talent, as is chess or languages with others. Likewise, during conversations with certain patrons, superior, independent minds –, government architects, deputies, experts, I would put together some ideas of my own –, other spheres opened themselves up. A writer, for instance, who would come more often and let his hair be washed with a certain blue water that lent a silvery gloss to his white mane, when I told him that I had found his latest article, they way it was done, interesting, retorted that he had horror of the terrible brutality implicit in the finding of the right expression, the birth of forms, and nobody would make him believe that the Almighty is gentle and twirls the spindle singing –: 'I am sure he bends his head and is startled to hear the boulders plunge.'

So I was bringing distant questions closer, and glanced inside me, yet what I saw there was amazing, there were two phenomena, it was sociology and the void. As soon as I discharged my business obligations, such as the payment of wages, the purchase of soap, tax evasion, the black market, nothing was left over that I might define as characteristic of my person. Sociology and the void! What was impulse was subdued by the State, the intellect toed the line of science, affectivity was laid claim to by the public welfare, recreation was decided by posters and travel bureaux, the indoors, by fashion, illnesses, by university clinics – analyzed, but still free were only the dreams. But all that was possible because the inner life, which I obviated in that way, found a substitute as soon as the self was blissfully evaded. Yet, time and again, I was shaken to see how the greatest minds – truly great – turned to sociology because they dared no longer to recognize themselves, their fullness, or lack of it, but most of all, their void ––, everything must be flush and thick, massif, inexhaustible, all square –, all these stigmata of nature and the corporeal, the century assumed for the spiritual and the productive as a matter of course; in its clumsiness, it could no longer tolerate a metaphysic of the void, a creed of the lethargics and the cataplectics (what would be the very assumptions of an identical description, an identifying definition of today's phenotype –), thus, sociology and the void –, at the most still the rupture colic, it must hurt, sometimes here, sometimes there, one feels it inside, the right shoulder joint, the legs too are no longer as they used to – thoughts, hogwash, but man is capacious, time disappears --: so ends the Mediterranean basin, from Acropolis, Athene Tritogeneia, wearing her scaly shield, contemplates the seas, her loneliness, her void.

In that direction too I laid my professional side. My salon is called 'Lotus' - an appeal to the sense of beauty, at the same time it sounds mythological - lotophagos, lotus-eater, whoever eats its fruit needs no other bread, he can hope and forget. Besides, my salon had an implicit selective character and conceptual delimitation: care of the body, including varicose veins - well, so far so good, that was also no haggle, but I refused to take it for the whole show, total care, unity of life, harmony. We all live something else than what we are. Here as there, fragments, reflexes; whoever says synthesis is already cracked. *Opportunities* - that was it! In the rhythm of the fortnight haircut or in the cycle of the four-week hair wash -: surface, be present only in the act, and then again submerge -: that was the ideological content of my salon.

That my salon belonged to a polis, was located in a place which formerly had been the showroom of Northern Europe, and now a model ruin, of devastated Carthago and of the disintegrating giant cities in the primordial forests of Saigon. Geology of peoples, the impact of history! From hanging gardens and lion gates to the grey border town through which travelled caravans from the East and the West. Storms of dust in summer, stinging nettles, the height of man, rising from the pavement, while at night, the grass was stealthily cut off the roads, along which formerly sleek motors had been speeding, fodder for the livestock kept hidden at home. A million of creatures, resembling human beings, are still among the wreckage, yet all jobless, behind nailed windows, rats under arches. A polity! Now, in winter, in the evening, I walk sometimes through the snow warily in the middle of the street, as the frost and gusts of wind chap the ruins.

Walk by the warming stations, refugee compounds, the makeshift huts, by the police stations that were keeping an eye on them, by district council offices, municipal lavatories, administrative abuses, organizational excesses, and behind them I was seeing the State, wholly immaterial, cachectic, with its transcendent services: it tracked down the rabbits and made sure that dental fillings were recorded; one had to take a four-week course to be allowed to cut out corns. With fiscal undercover agents and political informers, it squeezed the honest tradesman, the like of me, and by employing such methods, that made Scylla and Charybdis by comparison look like wild strawberries, it endangered the operation of the white and the black markets. In the concert halls, series of lectures, day and evening performances in three shifts, it processed beauty which fell into line: Philoctetes' bow and the song of the Fates behind the white lilac, and the fishers of Capri. Back to reality, to the electoral posters and the simple characters, the lavatory attendant had become esoteric, given the frozen water pipes, the 20th century relieved itself through the window. A nation of brothers, much of a muchness, this State! Furthermore, it organized conferences, set up commissions, those, in turn, organized conventions where the delegates in their turn took the floor: on the one hand/on the other hand, last but not least, fully and wholly. As already said, sociology and the void, but now there was an addition, though for that, I must go back.

A long-standing customer of mine, whose manicure by a new assistant I was supervising, related how his daughter – married and with two children – had paid him a visit again, after a long time. Charming person – we went along as if we had seen each other but the day before (yet, because of the hardships of war, it had been seven years) –, harmony and mutual recognition quite magic in character –, but she had done quite a good job of taking him for a ride, robbed him, charming in form but thorough in content, and now, said he, word for word: 'But women who have got children cannot be quite that well-behaved, they plunder and fill their backpacks on all highways; their minds engrossed in getting confirmation presents, and if they've got daughters, in matchmaking. The lion tears, the roe grazes, and this one here is maternal love, we enter the most sacred civic sphere.'

Unusual remarks! I who have no descendants, indeed, found them quite disconcerting! But my client had as soon reached a more conciliatory conclusion –, well, what do you want, he opined, it is the future, and we all serve it, indeed, it is life which excludes the solitary and subjects him to its eternal ends.

Life and its eternal ends – aha! – we were now at the salient point! In the presence of patrons one keeps one's private thoughts to oneself, one agrees with a patron, and then, with another, and so I limited myself to an approving mumble, but inside me, I was so agitated that I pretended I had to go on a business errand, and left the salon. Life – this spitoon in which all spit, cows, worms, harlots –, life which all devour skin, hairs and all, its utmost stupidity, its lowest physiological setting as digestion, as sperm, as reflexes – and still now, dished up as eternal ends, – but my client was right, here in the act lay the core of the generally received notion of the base of existence and which was effective in this race, of every notion, which philosophically speaking, had ruled reality in favour of the empirical sciences and had brought on the psychophysical tragedy, and which was now the final obstacle to the constitution of a new cultural sensibility, that after all these debacles, wanted to make allowance for a unification of spheres in the world to come.

Life – we are here at the basic concept before which everything stopped, the abyss into which everything precipitated blindly, having spoilt its values through neglect, gathered itself together, and deeply shaken, grew silent. But it seemed absurd to me to assume that the creator himself specialized in life, laid stress on, and went in for something else than his usual gimmicks.

That authority had indeed still other fields of operation, and cast its eyes from one thing to another and much farther from such an unclear special case. Life, provided one would like to get an overall view of its challenges and achievements, pointed to propagation as the centre of its good will, and which judging by experience, was to be managed simply and without looking. The first breaths of life were probably not without a faint light of the depths, and the old balloon manufacturer was perhaps taken aback by the effective albumen and his Indians, and all the possible jumps in the air which he could now let them begin again, – but for a cultural sphere made of the stuff of the purely spiritual experience, so distant from the vegetal, this notion of life was still largely primitive. Nietzsche did in fact say that the Greeks had become a great people because they recovered from their crises time and again with respect to their physiological condition, but there was something else that was conceived alongside it, something else that was imposed as a duty: the shaping of thought and the integration of the gods, – in its first month, the West, this bastard, and the rough sketch of all that, which it would become, stirred in their womb.

Life as city of mullatos: munching sugarcane, rolling rhum

kegs, deflowered at the age of ten and dancing cancan until the buttocks wag. But Europe missed the animal, stupid look and the hibiscus flower behind the ear. And someone else went up to it, an anti-mulatto, grabbed it by the throat, the Adam's apple, split open its narrow skull, sang atonal: a new balloon, an old sphinx: the intellect. The modern, living Europe ganged up against it, sought to break it in, reduce it to disciplines and methods, sanitized it, made it scientific, that means reliable, and concealed its lethal, bionegative traits. 'Only what is fertile is true' –,that is how they presented themselves, the ovaries are the greatest philosophers, and now they all moved to a one-family house and tended the West, they filled their eyes with lettuce in spring and mallow in autumn, Sundays they travelled eastward and westward from Greenwich, and there they shuffled their trotters. But behind, in the grey of things, there stood the other world, which glossed itself over fleetingly by means of space and time.

The West! Born of the Western Mediterranean, then terrestrially grown rich, – shipbow in Amalfi, a charcoal kiln in the Ardennes, – amphibian: scales, but at the same time, feet – : a dragon! The weight of dry land and the drive towards the sea. Primordial temple traditions, the egg motif of the world – overlapping rows of symbols, cross chains of thematic beads, Syrian apocalypses, Indo-Pacific sayings, Samoa and Persia, Olympus and Golgotha, Leda and Maria –: big culture retort, the last of the eight great solaria.

Profound and dissembling, fauns and sphinxes, local deities arrive over the old lunar bridges, but this narrow sea without tides brings monotheism, universalism, but also the premises of the destructive concept of synthesis, of law, of abstraction –, the terrestrial diversity and confinement could have never worked out the concept of cosmological unity. Poseidon-like –! Water, everything flows, – so, full of contradictions did the All-One begin, that it ended in the unreal, transcendental systems, then in us, in our void, in our inner shadows. In the end is the word, as it was at the beginning – was it at the beginning? Was the experience of the 'unreal' things at the beginning?

Yes, the remarks of the patron had taken me far – mallows and mulattos, real and unreal things, handed-over empirical and transcendental circumstances –, handed over, but by whom, and above all, whereto –, – the actual as real, the

11

actual as intellect, the actual as material myth – ineluctably lost in trains of thought which also had assumed something conventional about them, something professional, – frozen trains of thought that were just reverted to, time and again. The water and the words and the gods –, Tritogeneia that stares over the seas, her void, her being at a loss for an answer –, all but edges of steps –: and suddenly something happened which I could not explain even to myself, suddenly I began to love that winter, to feast on it, to chain myself to it. It breathed fire into me, – remain, reasoned I, let the snow lie eternally, let the frost have no end; afterwards, the spring stood before me as an encumbrance, it was no glass or clock manufactory, it roared, had something mauling about it, struck at every autistic reality, which I still sensed, but of which we have been deprived for ever. It would occur to nobody that behind those conflicting feelings lingered worries about milder weather, associated with the melting of the snow and the uncovering of corpses in the proximity of my house –, ah, but those were but ephemeral things! In an age, in which only the mass was allowed to count, the idea of an individual corpse was romantic. At a time when every personal life, every refinement, every productive oscillation would be branded as aestheticism and reactionary, I did not have to worry on account of some missing robots, curricula vitae, bottlenecks. Throughout I remained within the context of those times, had just to wait and see the results of their juridical hearings. Besides, I had long fostered the feeling, that given the situation in which the white peoples found themselves, it was by far more honourable to be fed in their prisons than in their clubs. No, – with the spring coming, something else was the matter: I would listen to the sound of the rain falling, which for months I had not heard, that sweet sound, I would stand by the window, see it fall upon the ground in the garden, that monotonous, silent ground, for which one had got no sense organs, even after having gazed at it that long, and which one did not grasp –, a new devastation would begin.

Morning was heaving itself, the cock was crowing, he crowed three times, he crowed flatly of betrayal –, but nobody was there any longer, either those who could have betrayed or the betrayed. All slept, the prophet and the times of prophecy; the Mount of Olives was wet with dew, the palm trees rustled in an impalpable wind –, a dove flew upwards, spiritus sanctus,

12

flitting its wings and the clouds took it up, it did not come back - the dogma was at an end.

Something like it I saw before me. Such an hour was there anew, an hour when something raised from the ground: the ghost or the gods or what had turned into a human being -, it dealt no longer with the demise of the individual human being, nor that of a race either, of a continent or a social order, a historical system, but something going far back came to pass: the absence of the future of an entire line of creation permeated the general feeling, a mutation - one tied to the ages of the Earth, to the hominids -, in one word: the Quaternary went backwards. Not dramatically, not as the end of a battle, rather atrophically through exhaustion, the exhaustion of the forms devised for the species. Here certain ideological drapes from the historical-political fund would still wrap several coming generations in the dazzling brightness of its low beams, in Asia, a few offerings would still be made to the witches, and certain prayers to the water rats before the temple, but there as here, it would all be play-acting, without deep faith, very see-through, very resilient, superficial and without any hope of fulfilment. What else should be there still, a few leftover solitary souls, some very lucid mind, deeply melancholic, that had been through a lot but kept silent -: the dogma of the homo sapiens, however, was at an end.

Of course there would be more eras, so called historical, this reptile 'history' would not make its exit without a sound -, over here too they would push and shove without any formalities. The next world view which one could envisage, would most likely be an attempt to bring together the mythical reality, palaentology and the analysis of the brainstem, but this too would be a stranger to unity and the tragic, no idea, no style would bloom on its path. It would be overshadowed by the awareness that it had failed utterly as a definition and explanation of mankind other than as cutting, as geographical and meteorological field, as the West's special case. It would push harder for the experience of the infinite than the present-day empirical-casuistic effort, but for us the primeval age is over. The psychophysical situation would be altered somewhat: the provoked life phenomena would compensate for a part of the naive and the raw, a few primitive reductions would materialize, a few deficiencies would be repleted by archaic rudiments, there would be a general feeling for the historical character of the present-day cultural consciousness, the relativity of its thesis, of its dimensions, its range further expanded and opened for debate, but an alteration of the ethnic-biological doings is no longer possible, attempts to cross over from measures to the transformation of reality will end in high spirits, impetuosity, exaltations, and probably into an ever clearer theoretical conceptualization of all this anecdotage.

And inside this world view, the five-star hotels will burst with overfilling, multipronged lifts will deliver at every door. The era of capitalism and of the synthetic life has only started. White, crocus-purple and brown painted lips will occupy the minds of ladies and signoras, 'pale coral' for golden hair, lilac for silver blonde, but only at the Tropics. The prolongation of life beyond any measure: glands will be traded, the liver made operational by means of filters, the antireticular cytotoxic serum (ACS) runs like sweat over the well-groomed flesh. From the Mena Hotel, the destination of many travellers on honeymoon, one gets the view over the proud symbols of an age-old culture; by the swimming pools, through which the filtered Nile flows, Bix Beiderbecke, the absolute jazz instrumentalist of both worlds, raises his saxophone to his chin and ends the rag-time with a tutti of the boldest overlaps, which at its climax remains suspended for one blink, and then fades. And at the Galle Face Hotel in Colombo and on the polo fields of Kandy the same goes on: the old orchid gentry and the new uranium clique: inside pokerface at the last bidding, outside poppy-red. The world will be made by the rich, and it will be done very well. The name of the piece is Aprèslude.

Should these lines, which are meant only for my friend O, who will keep them hidden, fall into the wrong hands, and somehow a posthumous reader would take them for the usual pessimism, this pessimism was but my weight and my attachment to the Earth. Or another may describe them as cynicism, admittedly there are a few results of the I, that may be appreciated only in this colour, it belongs to the sequence of perceptions that must be cold, otherwise it would turn trite, everybody knows that: it is ready to abandon a thought which it cannot express clearly. Nevertheless, other colorations were not strange to me –: hours filled with song, cantilenas, states of flux –: at times I would *hear* the Tropics: the buzzing of bees over the peonies and the cooing of the pigeons over the

14

blooms of bougainvilleas, and here in the North, too, there were strong feelings now and then -, were tears to give off a scent, I thought, it had always to be of phlox, the garden phlox, over which the thunderstorm would break at the end of summer. But one thing I have to concede on balance: in these lines there is more tension than bliss.

Tension -, yet no finale with trumpets and bassoon. On the contrary, I was imbued with a hypothesis of modern physics, which alone by its origins, suited a certain atmosphere. It was the nature of the Lotus-Land, where nothing happens and everything stands still -, the space with dimensions numerically even, in the distance of which the light persists after the extinction of its sources. The description comes from de Sitter. It reveals a strongly mathematical-physical imagination, but strikingly, it also recalls the trains of thought of other realms of the 'still desert of the Godhead', in which Eckhart saw the worlds emptying, and the Indian introversion, grounded in the certainty of one's own self, 'a wholly golden book am I, with no hands and feet am I, without being am I -', and such accusing sentences may also be found in an intellectual criminal, the like of Descartes, when he refers to a godhead that is ignorant of change and who always behaves in the same way. The godheads are indeed all over and done with, too many imponderables clung to them from cowardice, winks to Ananke, chancy necessity, and too little reference to effort, blueprints, recantation and play. But what impressed me most about this new designation was the connection with my salon: lotus, lotus-eaters -, whoever eats from its fruit needs no other bread, does not have to keep up appearances, he can hope and forget.

The situation hid many other possibilities and interpretations, yet to me one was obvious. The coming century would coerce man's world to face a decision, from which there is no escape any longer, no concessions, no winks, no black market, no emigration -, it will have to make up its mind. The coming century would allow for only two types, two constitutions, two forms of reaction: those who act and aim high, and those who keep silent and are on the watch for the transformation -: the criminal and the monk, nothing else besides. The orders, the brothers will once more rise before the extinction. I see new Athoses and new Monte Cassinos rising at the edge of waters and on cliffs -, black cowls wandering in silence, withdrawn.

Beyond the differences between the perceptible and the perceived, outside the chain of birth and rebirth. Through solitude, rites and the renunciation of the habitual, the autistic reality of the world expansion will go out, and in a calm, silent tat twam asi, that too are you, will the union with the lost world of things be consummated. Black cowls! The soul will once more close itself, will taste its lotus again and be able to hope and forget. Maybe – or maybe not. If that is not for me, perhaps for you. And if not for you, either, perhaps as clouds or doves before infinity, which in those winter hours spoke to me, before that player, the night visitor, who scattered this handful of earth out of his dream.

II. THE GLASS-BLOWER

A glowing summer and a city dying of thirst. Singed turf, trees smothered in dust. In the ruins, thirsting shapes, oozing salt through the pores, without any prospect of replacement, frail, looking for shade, – between faintness, circulatory disorders, and collapse.

Steppe-like living on the boulevards, – bustling bordellos and uniforms. The 8th Amurian Regiment, – peace garrison Lo-sha-go –, makes music in the open air, the trombones roar. The bars are filling up: Hawaiian trash and Siberian tainted blood. White vodka, grey whiskey, Ayala and Veuve Cliquot from unrinsed rummers. Gentlemen and gospodins tap-dance on the red glass floor, light effects from below, arm in arm with Helen-the-Nose, Sonya-the-Predator and Optic Alexandra (she's got a glass eye). The population looks on greedily through the windows: culture is forward-moving again, less murder, more song and sounds. The inner life of the defeated will also be taken in hand: a transatlantic bishop has arrived and mumbles: my brothers; – a humanist shows himself and says in a honeyed voice: the West; – a tenor brays: oh, sweet art --, the reconstruction of Europe is under way.

Europe will be pulled up by brains, by thinking, but the continent shudders, the thinking has its cracks. A famous writer from one of the Mediterranean countries writes to his Egyptian fan: 'the few will save the world' – the few – from what and in what way? No doubt that whatever created the world must have been first-rate, super, a hundred per cent, rolling on, certainly, in its unspeakable sphere, self-collected, watertight, drinking and eliminating its own substance, and maintaining an unimaginable balance, but there is something in us that does not join in, that gets annoyed, turns the outside inwards, asks questions, engages in discussions with like-minded people, in short, something that lacks the equanimity apparent in the things at rest, the things made of glass.

The urge to perfection that leads to suffering; hunches but never certainties. Were one to come to terms with the fact that one will not have enough to eat, will go thirsty, that the hands are not germ-free after washing them, that moods do not dissolve into harmony, that dreams sink without entanglement, that love changes and the change ends into forgetfulness – were one to learn all this, the second thermodynamic law of the existential, this apology of ruin, this universal of the soul, were we to lower our heads that we senselessly raise –, would this teaching lead us out of the wreckage, – did the abovementioned writer mean it, when he said that the few could save the world?

Those were the impressions and the thoughts with which I entered my salon one morning in July. The patrons were waiting, the gents wanted a good grooming, no tufts of hair hanging over the collar at the back, – the ladies wanted to be more beautiful: grey strands over the forehead, no specks on the skin (here we are at the chapter about the aversion to summer freckles, incomprehensible to me) – in short, I had to see that all was well, intervene, but inside me, I kept thinking my thoughts.

Giving instructions about the application of hot towels, offering advice concerning a broken fingernail, assessing the quality of combs, singing the praises of the birch balm, while inwardly thinking of destroyed and destructive things; I had turned this paradoxical thinking into a virtuosity. Today, while I was giving shape to a mop of hair with brilliantine – a mixture of benzoin, clarified lard and gardenias – I pressed on with my intellectual alternatives. Li Hung-chang had huge rotten fangs which he bared with his sinister laughter, a tall man with easy, jovial manners, – that was a linchpin, a linchpin in the Far East. Isvolski must have been short, his feet always wedged into patent leather shoes, his suit came from Savile Row, had white piping on the waistcoat, was shaking hands with averted eyes and always emanated a wiff of Violet de Parme. Then Caruso: the first act over, Gatti-Casazza, the administrator of the Metropolitan Opera House, calls on him and kisses him on both cheeks in earnest and full of dignity, every evening. Caruso fumbles for a vial of saline water, which he carries in every pocket; dresser and attendant stand on each side, one hands him a tiny glassful of whiskey, and immediately after, the other gives him a small glass of club soda, and then he will eat a quarter of an apple. Always stage-fright! The cleansing cold cream would be compounded by a chemist exclusively for him, on his own instructions, and had to contain no glycerine. Such were the times, and that leads me to the European question: *Is thinking a compulsion?* A tenor is an industry: estate manager, chefs, otolaryngologists, agencies –; mornings, at a thinking genius' place, a couple of sausage skins can be found on a plate, and the room is stuffy –, can it be believed that anyone would willingly harness himself to it?

Granted: panopticon, images, fragments coloured by questions! But the thoughts looking for coherence seem to me even more wanting. When an eye is cast upon Europe, one sees masses that think, back and forth, up and down, thinking on land and on water, aboard ships on their voyage, thinking out of primitiveness, as the apes climbing to the top of the trees, thinking out of skill, the way acrobats balance the balls, thinking in the four world languages and 22 Balkan dialects, with the result that nobody knows what kind of activity it is in reality, and what it is for. Were one to look, as I do, from an angle, into the thing, one would see a motley, in any case. By way of example, this moment, the many sloops before Yucatan, which helped the Spanish elementary hypertension to bleed so profusely, that it had to drop some of its European jewels from its crown, among them my homeland, – thus my system consists of the rustle of some stray palm trees by the Caribbean Sea, the whirring of a few bowstrings and various coolie castes from another place. The cayman too, dripping with guano because the white heron lay in wait for fish on its scaly back, and red parrots. Lava and gaily glimmering rivers. More remote flora and fauna, Lucculan and prophylactic: when the giant locust devastates the fields of sugar cane and the phylloxera compromises the Mosel grape vines, when the Brazil rubber is impermeable and the waterproof is invented –: all give shape to my hours. When the gentleman desired more hair on his head, I would treat it with benzoin. I rubbed harder, sang the praises of the solution doubly, pretended to have noticed it growing already here and there, light fuzz, a willing epidermis, joyfully opened pores. We discussed the matter, he as a wistful idealist, I as a specialist. 'Has the future already passed?' –, both recalled that title of an article in yesterday's paper, about an unearthed skull of a Negro which had the traits of today's hypermodern man: stunted set of teeth, more brittle than the present, no grinders at the back, a high forehead (attributed to hair loss) –, 'less simian than any modern skull,' 15,000 years old, strewn along the South African coast, 'premature birth of the European', 'gone under in the harsh environment', 'what a surprise for the archaeologists', 'overdevelopment of the Caucasian type,' – expanded brain volume, too, – hence probably an intellectual life, processed impressions of the surroundings, poetry, – bulls instead of roses, conch cadences instead of radio –, the puzzles increased.

In this context I may mention a gentleman who patronized my establishment on a regular basis. A truly distinguished figure, his profession, however, remained unclear to me, perhaps a diplomatist, or an artist, who nowadays kept to himself. A societal observation: the times were such that rapprochements in conversation became possible between separate status groups, and the trades, as well, hardship levelled all, the future preoccupied us equally, new worries confronted us and new wars threatened. Thus an elegant man, always tiré à quatre épingles, widely travelled, lordly globetrotter, regularly on the 1st of August, would hurry from Dauville to Biarritz, and had been riding in the famous coaches with the silvery top hats from London to Ascot for seven years running, dressed in a light grey tailcoat and wearing a hat of the same colour, with a black band round the crown; he had also been very much immersed in such sports as cricket and hunting with hounds. I shall further reproduce one of our conversations:

'When I now come to you through what used to be streets, and on the way see the vicious, pinched and at the same time empty faces, those loathsome faces, it always occurs to me that it's sad to think that we are related, but within the historical world, how consistent and true! A nation wants to make world politics but cannot abide by any agreement, wants to colonize but has no command of any languages, wants to assume the role of middleman by going on a Faustian quest, – every one believes he has something to say, but none can talk, – no distance, no eloquence, – they call elegant apparitions conceited asses, – they install themselves as a mass over all, their views come with fat behinds, – they don't know how to fit in any society, they stand out in any club, – for three decades they had, I suppose, even money, but not enough for well-tended lawns, – have you read what Bülow recorded about the interiors at Friedrichsruh: no beautiful pictures, no big library, no mention of ceilings, Gobelins tapestries, oriental rugs: Homer's sun never smiled on that house, and the

20

splendour of the Italian Renaissance, which had cast at least a ray of light upon some of the castles in the North of Germany, such as Tegel, or upon the house of Goethe, did not reach it. I should add that it was all bleak and bare like the potato fields round Fehrbellin, after the stalks had been burnt. Individualists, in the provincial sense, with nothing to satisfy them, bad losers, – when one walks through the streets here now, the dust is blown about and settles on everything, indeed, but it is not the light, white dust of the Mediterranean lands that covers your Chrysler with snow, it is not bright, auspicious ash from brittle herms and worn-out Aphrodites, strewn over roses and oleanders in a last breath.'

'A world of constraints, this whole political world, today a world under the sway of the magic wand from the Antarctic to the Erzgebirge: uranium, pitchblende, isotope 235! Far- and deep-going neurosis! Zoon politikon – a Greek mistake, a Balkan idea! Whoever pleads in favour of the political world, can do it only out of a whim. When you think how many individual fates were affected by it, and moreover, destroyed, because a uniform for a great monarch was not on hand in time and so cancelled a visit, – or that a launch showed up an hour late because of some snag, and as a result, the emperor's mood turned foul by the time the parley was to begin, would you then have second thoughts about this whim? If you knew how many rows of coincidences are needed for an Empire to pursue its policies just for three generations, its foresight, perhaps rationally arrive at, so that it might remain consistent to some extent through all embassy palaces, enterprises, regattas, reviews, referenda, what series of happy coincidences of unimaginable variations of this arrangement are necessary, you would keep wondering. If afterwards you would sound deeper and see what the content of this political world is like in reality, namely the progress, for instance, from the wheel to the guillotine, this humane progress, which without a hitch at the beginning, faciliated the first European model genocide during the French Revolution –; or the importation of African slaves into tropical America through the services of a Jesuit father, in order to spare the native Indians –, but how afterwards this slave trade stood sponsor to the whole Western civilization, that is, through the so-called Assiento-rights which Madrid sold for thirty years at a time to the Genoese, the French, the English, – from these dingy little ship bellies the gold flowed, treasures flowed, Picadilly and la Ville lumière flowed, – the potato flowed; – and then the bombastic abolition of that slavery, the arm-wrestling over the niggers, and now the North Borneo Company spouts contract coolies and kan-akas from similar little ship bellies into the tin mines and the rubber plantations of the Insulinda, lying the groundwork for concerts in the Albert Hall and for the happy splendour of summer residences --: a mistake! And if retrospectively I add that the blowpipe is superior to the Colt inside the political world because it does not betray the killer, and the dugout is not threatened by submarines, at most by the snouts of crocodiles --; and finally, as a prognostic, I beg you to let the essence, the inner aspect of the white colonization appear before your mental eyes: firstly the whip across the dappled blood and the petroleum on the mosquito puddles, then tar and steamrollers for the highway from Balboa to Colon, and in the third generation, the coloured gentleman playing his game of baseball at the Washington Club, dividing the world into remarkable and shocking, and going fishing, swimming, shoot-ing, hunting in the mayonnaise pool from Palm Beach to Havana – do you follow me?'

I followed him, and in fact, I was spellbound. In the same way, little Pfordte of the Atlantic Hotel in Hamburg, former waiter, had occasionally joined the highest of its guests in their discussions, and old Pinnow had not only produced claret and Lacrima Christi from below the stairs on good and bad days, but he had also had human ties with the great old soloist in the forests of Saxony. So it was with this gentleman: I took his remarks as tokens of recognition for my services meant to satisfy him. He went on:

'Do not think, dear Sir, that I have no regard for the great hours of history. It is half past eleven on the 2nd of September 1899, with a steady hand, Kitchener sticks the field glasses back into their case, the battle of Omdurman had been won, 30,000 dervishes dead or wounded; the Mahdi defeated: fourteen years had the Sirdar prepared for this hour, and England with him, Gordon is avenged, all very well, I understand that. In the same way, at Königgrätz, where Moltke waves his silk handkerchief and the Empire is born – well, it did not last long, but I don't mind: fine! Still, in between, modern physics and old religion, existentialism and palaeon-tology have directed our attention to transmundane perspectives, have found a language for infinite spaces, distances, eternities, and disasters, as well, and here we are to cling to this one continent, or two, to fasten our whole existence to this overhasting and fleeting floor of the Earth, to keep the few hours of our lives at the disposal of a government apparatus, to allow a State to order us about, to be hard-working and efficient - how full of contradictions all this is!'

'Do not think, my dear Sir, that you could confirm or contest my views. Rest assured that for me the consensus omnium is hardly more than a cabbage white that flies over all the kitchen gardens! In case you would like to hear the maxims of my life, they are the following: 1) Discern the situation. 2) Reckon with your deffects, rely on your resources and not on your slogans. 3) Do not round off your personality but each of your works. Blow the world as glass is blown, as the breath into a pipe-stem: the stroke with which you detach everything: vases, urns, lekythoi, - that stroke is yours and it is decisive. 4) Fate meddles only with mediocrities, what is alive leads its existence on its own. 5) If someone accuses you of aestheticism and formalism, look at him with interest: it is the caveman, it is the sense of beauty of his cudgels and aprons that talks through him. 6) Occasionally take some bromide, it stabilizes the brainstem and the irregularities of the affects. 7) Once more: discern the situation.'

He concluded: 'If you let it affect you, it is part of the situation that you see around, the kind of people who have not yet found the way to express themselves and cannot find it by any means - because of the State-regulated destruction of all substance. If a playwright wants to see his play performed, he must create conflicts, but there is only one modern conflict: that between the State and freedom, so the author has no alternative but to get his work mounted with the help of rabbit hutches, or stolen milk cans, or hotel suites. When you find such patronymics as Burckhardt and Hallström in a modern novel, it makes you sick, they are all just plain Müllers and Schulzes, and what happens to them is common. The conflict between individuals has died out, as has the centrifugal expression. By sticking a beard on his face, the actor may avail himself of the so-called dramatis personae to mask his existential monotony. So he raises his right arm, and then his left arm, and that passes for expression, while the waving of both extremities stands for rage and creature writhings, but it is only body-snatching and ostentation. The man of today has one characteristic trait: he is centripetal – perhaps a way of protecting the core, he holds his hand in front of the candle, he lives in a screened light.'

'Man stands in quite a different place from his syntax, he is far ahead of it. The man of today reckons neither with the past nor with the future. The sentence which he is writing must include everything, or perhaps the paragraph, while in the case of the painter, it may be the picture; but what extends beyond that is incapacity, and relies on the good will of others. The artist is the only one who will get through the things and will decide on them. All the other types will go on wetting the problems, for generations, for centuries, until they come to a halt and decompose, until – in evolutionary terms – their brains change and nature intervenes – thus an inhuman under- taking, unworthy of man. And so I said: the stroke on the pipe, the stroke which detaches everything, – and so I said: the glass-blower.'

Up to this point, the gentleman from Ascot. Perhaps my rendering is too tediously long and rambling. But when a history of the early thornless olive tree can be printed in two volumes, brought out by the Heidelberg Academy of Science, and many other works on the dark-brown eye pigment of the flour moth ephestia, as well as an encyclopaedia on the extracts of bluebottle pupae, one may be permitted quietly to take note of such calmly conveyed views. I had long lived expanding my brains through reading, making notes, and by aides-mémoires, into which I have now crammed a portrait of that gentleman, as well. How hot the days were! But I had known other days, too, mild summers, with flower beds of fantastic colours, one was silent and the eternities passed by, everything came together in silence and dream, and one caught sight of the distinctions. It happens now, too, as I reflect upon some of the remarks reproduced above, with their occasional inconsist- encies.

One could in fact see that earlier, into many a distance. All lay already very close together, at times all the sails lay one next to the other: those of Salamis and the Mayflower, and those of the regattas at Cannes. The rose followed its own fragrant path, and filled with all its umbels but a glance: from Asia, through the gardens of Midas, elbow-high on the marble

24

floors at Cleopatra's feasts, and trailed on, fainter scent and fragrance, became the black rose in Findland, the rose of the dead elsewhere and the oil rose somewhere else – and now the whole path filled but a glance.

To glance back! Still the glance forward also knew what the hour had struck. It saw the maze of paths but would not disentangle them. Even in the wilderness of this destroyed city, the heat and no water, the thoughts with no companions to share them with, the monologues of which not one was new, – even when all this should have compelled it to some extent to reach differentiated results – it always discerned only one: either that everything was nothing or everything was something. But it could not key its predisposition, its mood, its optic recorder on the latter without realizing that it too amounted to a complete dereliction of values inherent in the individual system, to a promiscuity, a levelling of forms which was identical, both originally and theologically, with the void.

The intellectual fluid had assumed something catastrophic, it belonged to the realities that had been called 'inner' during past centuries, but which now were spent, empty, collapsed – a pair of scraped cat's skins crumbling in some corner. And the 'outer', which sent forth certain signs and perhaps came closer at one time, had no depth yet, and probably it hadn't got any, it assumed other dimensions, to which nobody had yet forced his way.

The fluid, which saturated this continent intellectually, was long known to be without an outlet, nevertheless, its countries went full blast to restore it. It is in this sense that I asked earlier: is thinking a compulsion? And now I ask further: have the things any earnestness about them? Do they have engraved traits, rules and regulations, letters of marque and seizure –, no, they are an alien world, closed, indifferent, with cold shoulders. How can meaning be derived from that, in order to attain a structural unity through its intellectual manipulation, to press on with it, complementing, classifying, juggling concepts which then must be agreed upon, proven to be true? On the other hand, who can believe in earnest that any identity can be experienced by this method? Which are the traits of whoever claims to find his necessity in this?

They are the traits of a local heavyweight about whom it is obvious above anything else that precisely he does not need an identity, that moreover, he evades every important answer on principle. To ask him for an answer seems to him to lower his status. This thinking will not in the least answer what life, or heredity, or the essence of matter is; it is self-centred, it mirrors the questions, as for eyes, it is blind. Self-satisfied, it lets all to look on, and every onlooker knows precisely that something quite abnormal is going on here, but nowhere is any strength left to stop it, for it presupposes the will to allow a new material reality to arise with sublimated mental requisites and a genuine ritual of identification, but the race is too exhausted for that.

As a result, I had often thought of emigrating and seeking out a continent where another kind of thinking would be prevalent. My notes referred to Lhasa -, by the way, its conquest by the English in 1904 had been one of their far-sighted political rounds. There, on seven yellow silk pillows, sits the Tobden Lama, the King of Words, the Ocean of Wisdom. Prayer mills with or without bells, prayer cylinders with rotating handles, prayer wheels with a circumference of up to 5 metres, in houses specially built for them, prayer machines driven by water and wind ruled over the continent. Conch trumpets, metre-long trumpets that had to be carried by four men, kettledrums, clarinets over a quarter of the world. Chinese, Mongols, Buriats, Indians, Turkmens from Lake Baikal, from the Caucasus, from the Volga, from Siberia gravitated towards it. All the caravan roads converge there. Om mani padme hum: Oh, you jewel in the lotus, amen - all throw themselves down in the dust. Here the things are on the outside, they are not so oppressive, nobody includes himself in a so-called context, horse dung or yak turds will be gathered, and fruit fallen from the trees, but nothing in the way of a structural whole, rather for fuel. Yet: discern the situation! Yet, I told myself presently, the orchestra of the Lamas makes an extremely shrill music, - even for someone coming from a country so tolerant of music as I do, it would be unbearable. Day and night drum roll call and monkish chant at work, on the move, in the pastures, in the bazaars, kettledrum symphonies, religious collegiate syncopations, it must bring unpredictable grace but it would be too much for me. Cosmetically, too, that is, they never wash with water, only smear their faces and always with butter, I could never join them, given the nature of my salon, dedicated to modern hygene and coming under the jurisdiction of the Department of Public

Health. 'Jewel in the Lotus' –: advert balm for my salon, but actual affinities with Karakorum, impossible! Thus I found myself faced with two contradictory vegetational forms of thinking, and I was not ready for, nor capable of either.

In my quest for continents I had also cast a glance upon the religions that caused Nietzsche so much suffering, indeed. How out of date was it all! Here, too, flora and fauna have moved on. There were religions without the concept of god, without any of those ideas of divinity to which Europe jumped so controversially, for which she had so wilfully vied. Among them, there was the greatest, Buddhism, which knew neither god nor immortality nor individual soul – those experiences, on which the earlier inner life, in our case, took hold, they too became a regional mood with monologues, dialogues, offerings, benefices, and as a whole, is nowadays as wistful as the glance cast back to a life spent on the stage. If thus the holy of holies was meant for mankind, why then was it so changeable, full of contradictions, so much in need of thesis and antithesis, born of a rock, one time, and of a virgin , another time, how on the other hand, was doubt at all possible, from what background did it emerge –, given the situation, it is only too understandable that nowadays man no longer attaches importance to what was once rooted in faith. And finally, that very idea, which had been so much quoted everywhere and always with such emotion, lost its magic, and had to be rigged out with historical missions of supposedly quite primary importance, the idea of *Humanity*: in our proximity, there have been superior cultures without any humanity: the Egyptian, the Hellenic, that of the Mayas, that of Yucatan, and the latter with a music of sublime sadness, the music of a mature, overripe people aware of their decline, a music of pure gold, in short, if my glance fell on mirror-like reflections, or yak turds, or scholastic controversies and historical missions, everywhere it saw only cat skins, and if at the beginning I had said euphemistically that the continent was shaking, it was however much more a tectonic quake, the genuine symbols of which were the ruins around us, – the Royal Air Force had presumably dropped nothing.

I am sure that the above-mentioned facts have long been known to mature people among the educated circles, they will find them banal, but I had to go through my overviews slowly. That cost me additional physical effort which I want to mention. I remember an incident from my youth. I was standing in the harbour of Santos. On my left, there was the Guaruja Hotel, its gambling rooms had been closed down several months before, the gambling, though, moved into one of the neighbouring villas. The beach lay deserted, ebb tide, a few cars were racing on the instantly drying sand, it was that hard, and on my right, a German steamship was leaving the quay; for a while it was still in the estuary, then out, on the open sea, and beyond was Europe; I was thrilled.

The steamship had polo ponies aboard, which would race and trot in Surrey and perhaps before that, at Frohnau, as well. I had a mental picture of those places, the exquisite team members on the ponies and on the turf, one was as handsome as Adonis, another as superhuman as Holofernes, the third as unconcerned as Diogenes, nabobs from cities built round wells, and others from cities of high-rises built of concrete, and then the ladies, my area through and through, I smarted them up, smell of carnation toilet water, clouds of incense extracts, summer hats: straw with a rose of black tulle, – those nonchalant little things that matter so much to us. Parasols, gaudy like parrots, jackets of wonderful vanilla-ice-cream-coloured balloon silk were flown in on board an airplane. But behind those fields, other scenes unfolded: an evening on the banks of the Nile, where the Club of the 'incomparable living' was having a feast, the Egyptian lady dropped the pearl into the wine and seven dromedaries were made to lie down, loaded with mellons. Then Provence, the courts with the troubadours, the parties where violets were tossed; – then the Greek feasts: handsome sileni, vats full of red wine, hands loaded with fruit, mouths full of grapes, everything in motion, Venus laid down the sea scallop and a shepherdess grabbed a flute –, and while the images changed and passed by, one after the other, I saw over my continent a swing of staggerers, a continent wholly crowded with snares and twists, with downfalls, the individual shapes turned formless inside me, certainly a tendency to regression, the unconscious revival of earlier states of existence: to become water, to seek out the lowest level which all avoid, – a wholly anti-European tendency, close to the Tao.

An intense, frantic force was at work inside me, pushing me to consummate the direct union with the world of things, to let the stigmata of the centuries subside, to arouse the buried unity of being, drowned in an infanticide, and to

28

consign the western phantoms of space and time to oblivion. There, on the beach of Santos, at an European's! I had read that it was Plato who came with the idea that all inside us is recollection, that our life is not what we saw and did, but rather what lay in us, and we were meant to allow it to surge in images and thoughts, and to lend it expression. That, too, a Greek idea, but entirely contrary to the above-mentioned Balkan idea! It was a doctrine of primal experience, that doctrine under the plane trees where he lingered with Phaedon, those white trees, harbingers of the spring where one could rest, the beasts quench their thirst, and moisten one's own lips to the chorus of cicadas. I often experienced such states of anamnesis, even long after I had left Santos and the surrounding fever holes. Yes, occasionally, I could bring them about in me, and they became the elucidation side of my existence and its inner reviews.

You must have nothing to do, patrons or acquaintances would say whenever, carefully, I broached those things with them, - of course I had nothing to do, what was there for me to do, the business to pay the rent and buy on the black market -, but what to do with this overwhelming mankind where, in the presence of its historical idea, my own idea stood a chance in 20 million, - what to do, - but when I suddenly see the sails over the seas and waters, white, brown, multi-coloured, of Salamis, the Mayflower, and possibly some on Lake Titicaca, from the early times to the regattas of Cowes: was that nothing, - that, I felt distinctly, was what I had to do.

One must be honest, whatever the risk, à propos, what are the risks, death is something beyond the human to be degraded to the level of risk -, so one must be honest and that is why I proved to myself that the only fragments of the spiritual of which I was fully aware were the disintegration which suspended the hour and staked everything on one card and played that card calmly at first, then recklessly, unconcerned about loss or gain. And hereby I found a new connection to the gentleman from Ascot, his glass-blower, and a paranthesis which he would insert and which I often noticed, but its painful meaning became clear to me only gradually. It went as follows: - 'All this is valid only in the context of my words' -, that is to say, what he meant by those words concerned only him, alone, the circumstances were not such as one could still speak for the others, or to the others, the sentences barely traversed a room, one brought forth the images for oneself alone.

Out there, the world in its intellectual disintegration, and in here, the I with its historical misfires. And then the doctrine of the plane trees and the high aesthetic of the glass-blower: the incandescent stream and then the stroke upon the pipe, a breath – and then the fragile walls covered by shade and light. 'Isn't it all but the key in which we play when looking for the gods' – the voice of another called across, one of the present heavyweights, one worthy of a back glance and whose work permitted us to believe that not all destinies are at an end. You step back into the shadows, but something from you will linger on. And if in your case too, it is only vases and glasses that the stroke detaches, and not the deep reliefs and the rows of characters, if in your case too, one deals only with humble pieces, you too hold onto the land to which your dreams are drawing you and where you find yourself to quietly fulfil the things that have been imposed upon you.

III. PTOLEMY'S DISCIPLE

Winter is coming again, the colour and the silence of bronze spread over the city, and the spiders emerge. The light glides off the plumage of swallows; whoever has got some piece of ground is now harvesting his garden, the streets smell of tubers and the tobacco is hanging from balconies. Soon, the stormy weather will come to stay, frost, hunger and contagious diseases will trample us with their hooves; the farsighted City Council has already augmented the number of gravediggers, and the flower shops are expecting a booming trade in wreaths.

'A stork under the skies knows its appointed time' - I don't want to know less than this deserter; 'a turtle-dove and a crane are aware of their time' - I don't want to be less lucid than those winged creatures. Therefore I say that the only thing that keeps us on our feet is the black market, it is excellently organized, and the prices are almost stable, it is the monetary reform both in a speculative and a moral sense: looking at the pound of sugar and the tin of coffee, one knows what one is working for, ora et labora. Among my patrons, none of those who get one thing or another in that way think otherwise than I do, and even my employees more often than not produce bits of something extra from their pockets. The only ones who live on their allotted rations are obviously the public organs, the district councils and the agencies for price control.

The material bases of our existence are of recent date. The Chesterfield first appeared between the world wars, made by Liggett and Myers; the first blended cigarette came forth in the shape of the Camel in 1913 - the Duke Trust. The same year, Bohr's new and sensational theory of the atom was made publicly known. On the 20th July 1920, the opening of the Panama Canal, sixty kilometres long, a hundred metres wide, the Atlantic is twenty metres higher than the Pacific, and the tide rises 58 metres at Colon and only 6 metres at Balboa, whence the difficulties. In order to be commercially viable, some 50 ships must pass through it daily, but then the pineapples of Honolulu and the pearls of Macassar reach the

Seine two months earlier. Insulin in 1922, the sulphonamides in 1935. In 1922 numerous Negro bands migrated from New Orleans: Alexander's jazz march up to our gates. All the blue dye in Europe since Caesar's bellum gallicum had been made of woad, Thuringia being the main region for its cultivation, but the indigo drove it off the market, the first synthetic dye made of tar, it was in 1900. My father used to tell that whenever they went visiting in the country, rice was served as the ultimate refinement, it was the newest gourmet dish; it was the time when in the country, mail was delivered once a week, – today it is the same, so a certain uniformity is spreading over the Earth, and sociology and the philosophy of culture fall asleep like premature babies. 1947: while the gypsy tribes from both hemispheres were choosing a new ruling family at the Shrine of Saint Sarah in Saintes-Maries-de-la-Mer, the old royal houses of the Kviek and the Sarana had finally exterminated each other, and in Chicago, the four goats that had survived at Bikini, were under observation. As I was emerging from nothingness, the Manchus were still ruling over China, and in Berlin, the shops were still open on Sundays; three dozen cables were linking Europe and the USA, but someone, who came back from the Russo-Japanese war, mentioned in passing that the Kirghiz and the Tartars were still singing songs about Tamerlane. What I want to say by all this is that we are in a state of flux, and its waters are slowly running, impenetrable in many ways; today it takes a spiritual turn: no causality, no psychology and no pensions, even animals experience the adverse: the cats have grown weary of rats, and the buntings shake off the worms. On the other hand, a certain consensus has been reached as far as shades of cinnamon, ginger and amber for shawls and handbags in this low season, the ear lobes will be heavily adorned, and the rouge baiser and After Shave lotion are once more available in adequate quantities amidst the ruins.

In those critical autumn weeks, under the influence of certain states of suspense and of a large bed of zinnias in the Botanical Gardens, it occurred to me to sell my salon, change my life and move to some lake, a flat expanse of dark waves, big enough to sustain my gaze, to prolong it to the distant shores. Man wants to see all together, to hell with the fragmentation of cities, driven by the demarcation mania, the eternal displays of objects in shop windows, junk shops, alluring kiosks, to hell with the troublesome turns and the never-ending squeezing and dodging in the traffic to yield to those fish-faced, bull's-eyed, shark-tailed limousines, - man wants to feel the unity of apperception, to live in it, to take pleasure in it, because it alone confirms his origins and his hour, and the countryside promised all that: for days I saw that lake before me, its unspoilt looks, its simplicity, its silence, its colours. That was mostly the mood, but there were additional syntactic and semantic motives. Whenever I had looked about through the vocabulary of my people, I had long discovered many words which I could have never coined on my own: holy, snowcap, starlit, everything vertical would not have occurred to me, - for flat, water, horizontal situations I could have contributed a few, as for the subconscious, drowsiness, for things associated with Pan, the god of the Greek country-side, for honeycombs, gardens, the noon hour. Words from the steppe had always moved me deeply. The skies are a bow and fate is an arrow, and Allah is the archer, as the saying goes in Islam. On the whole, the Asiatic cut very often across my individual perspicacity, the most genuine aspect of which I always felt to be the amorphous, the ambivalent.

The Asiatic, the East, its cruelty, its immense splendour, its thirst for power and its resignation, its dust which moves across deserts as wide as the seas, and the white marble of which the Mogul palaces had once been built, built and then crumbled, - yes, everywhere ruins, sunken into the earth, a self-absorbtion which fostered the now forgotten wisdom, in my own field: the yoga techniques, the Chinese acupuncture which also knew the early therapy of the solar plexus, the in-fluence of every hidden point and centre that condition the tone of our lives, vitalistically superior to the modern Euro-pean reflexology, which focusses mostly on the capacity for work and finds legitimacy exclusively in the increase of the industrial output, - there, the Jordan flowed from which other baptisms emerged, and down there, the Ganges where other pilgrims knelt, - my lake was hemmed in by all those waters, it flowed over into the Mongolian distance, mostly unruffled, only in the autumn would it fling foam between the reeds, and the tenant farmers would row out and slowly fish with their creels.

Temptations and everywhere water lilies, looking almost like fish -, Titan immersed in his dream! Nevertheless, I can explain only in a roundabout way what made me remain in the city. The starting point were the Zoological Gardens, the big cities are in direct competition with one another about wildlife reserves, aquaria, insectaria, everyone can observe at leisure what time does to organic life. But inside consciousness, as I had discovered, things were different, – but why was it set to conceal and to deny them? I had studied the most important of the major modern novels in which Europe was seeking and recognizing herself, GROWTH OF THE SOIL and THE RAINS CAME, but the conclusion was always the same as in FAUST, Part II: honest work and service to the community, there, in Norway, here, in Ranjipur. Wonderful to have such deep feelings and not to have to put up with the current situation. Idealism, faith in the future, confidence in life were entrenched behind that line, it was the borderline concept, water, the outline of palm trees in the desert. But groups of people had appeared for whom life had no longer a central, an existential weight, it was not fulfilment, the fairest of the greatest father's daughters, it had no more wings to carry it either upwards or downwards, those groups bore it on their own, they had to, that was their weight, it was the last and only thing for which they felt deeply, and it became clear to me that this was the modern Europe in which I wanted to remain.

That was my offering for many things in a place where I could no longer make any. All that has got a sense of decency lays its own hour on the altar, the gods do not accept borrowings from strangers. In this I followed the gentleman from Ascot: the gift must have content, the moral is to lend expression to that content, the talent is to present it in an interesting way, – I knew of no other cosmic conditions. This limitation was of course time-bound in the extreme, perhaps there are even other times, or somewhere else perhaps there are times with far broader horizons, immense inward and outward radiations, loftier arches and domes, but not here and not now. Smyrna was Homer's cradle and the grave of Tantalus, but in different generations –, the second was later, and the devil take the hindmost.

The business, the high-rise, the metropolis blocking out lakes and forests: I have rooted my life here, and here, too, I wanted to dispose of its end with precise instructions: half of my ashes to be dispersed in the September wind, and the other half to be saved in an empty tin of Nescafé! Heightened, provoked life, – tensions, extracts! To stay with the things, discern them, and then blow them out – and at certain hours, that seemed to me very easy to carry out. There was a jet of notes about things, details that I studied, and then sent them flying. That was life! And here, at the destination, in the stability of space, in the midst of employees and patrons, the things would untwist! Within the social world, – my God, this social world, – whoever could juggle and wear masks, kept slipping through its network! I would smear and knid, yet I looked round, taking all in, filling my hours, and I went on transforming myself. A lady in black, intent on wending her way abroad, asks for the curly American hairstyle; the hair dryer is lowered over her head in no time, – tel est mon plaisir –, the hands are doing what it is required for the honeymoon but the mind stamps out the biological glut, ravages the petrified, ignites the blaze. What are the doctrines, what is history – bons mots, arabesques, curlicues in the panta rhei! Little turns of phrase: Kublai Khan moves his capital city from Karakorum to Pekin; the sinicization of the Mongols, the victory of observatories and of sericulture over the huntsman's tent made of panther hides, grandfather Genghiz Khan turns in his grave, his grave in the withered grass of Tartary! Little turns of phrase: the shadows of the battle of Plassey, which Clive gave in 1757, chasing the Gauls out of Bengal once for all, those shadows that stretch out from the Khyber Pass across the homeland of the snows and down south, to the jungles of the tigers, dissolve into uncertainty, and the big ruby of the last imperial crown returns to Rangoon where it came from. Here a successful adventure, there a misunderstood command, – patrols, squadrons, divisions of ghosts, generals, governors, Knights of the Order of the Bath, of the Order of the Golden Fleece, Knights Commander of the Order of the Maltese Cross, bow, give the salute, fall à toutes les gloires, and lastly, two civilians slowly descend a flight of steps, the great staircase of a great castle, enter the park, stop in front of the parterres of heliotropes and the trout ponds, they stand and are silent – two Englishmen, alone and tired.

No, not on the lake, – it is here that the fog lifts, it is here that the curtain rises from riddles and the night. The peoples migrate, and the gods with them: from his African Olympus in the rainy forests of the Sudan, Vodu dismounts in Haiti, and the Madonna from Rome, at Port-au-Prince, as

Maitresse Etilée. Over the Kashmiri passes, the Indians mix with the Hellenes; through the defile of Isère, the Carthaginians overpower the Seven Hills; up the mountains and down the slopes, drive and flashes, then smashed skulls and bones, strictly speaking, only the vultures are steadfast! The Roman emperors flit straight out of this life; the Yuan dynasts would be soft boiled with poison and dagger; the Merovingians would tattoo each other with murders and vengeance, the Romanovs would seek direct contact with bombs in carriages and shots in theatre boxes --: only the vultures!

Nonetheless it was not an exclusive playground for gruesome feelings that I was fostering, comments on sport and business, too, quietly found their way, the entire reality rose, sank and played its rounds. India, which before had attained world mastery only in hockey, was weakened considerably by the partition. The Salt Lake in Utah, on which a 3-litre and 550 HP contraption had wiped out all national and international records, could be speedily reached in the new three-tiered car, named Astradome, of the Yankee Clipper. The new golf bag with its own carriage for the caddy followed. At the Kentucky Derby, the famous race for the roses, because the winner is adorned with a big garland of red roses, would put an abrupt end to the career of Assault, the little wonder from Texas – and who owned that crack on the racecourse of Churchill Downs in the country of 'Blue Grass' –: Elizabeth Arden-Graham, the cosmetics queen from New York, whose products I was selling.

It is nine o'clock in the morning, my glass doors start revolving, the ladies and gentlemen arrive, I lead them to their chairs, they ask for their favourites, men or young women who have always waited on them. I act as a go-between. That is handicraft, manual work, but even if one lets Hans Sachs out of it, Spinoza in any case ground lenses, worked with bellows, and nonetheless, produced a doctrine which impressed the Olympian. My branch is as old as the world, Job's third daughter was called Keren-happuch, that means little rouge pot, it glorified cosmetics, and Poppaea, Nero's wife, always took one hundred she-asses with her on her travels, and daily bathed in their milk mixed with myrrh and corn – the equivalent of the lait virginal of the 18th century. Alcohol was yet unknown, and milk and wine were loaded with fragrances. Here, too, my compensatory world was ruling: the kohl of

36

today's Egyptian women is the mestemet of the old, the black sulphur antimony, loaded on a stick and spread on the eyelids, and then the eyes were closed gently. Thus, the recurrence of the same! In the material world, there are associations, recurrence of motives, while in the world of commerce it is the eternal transaction, and in the social world, what rules are the myths of retrospection: the masses had indeed formed the third estate everywhere, long ago, though they have not governed everywhere as long, – in short, far and wide there was law and scope for the expressive-archaic sphere, its autolysis, its maceration into nothingness, and so enlightened, to reach for the images in the plane trees of memory.

In a city where there is nothing but fleecing and indigence, where crimes make sense and the prison cells are in short supply, other intellectual needs come to light than in those lands where sitting in a red velvet armchair between two sage bushes in his garden, the Shah slurps a nectarine, or where a lord in tails raises his arms to the back of his head to fasten hook and eye on the blue and scarlet ribbon of the CMG Order, or on the beach of a scabious-coloured sea, where the green umbrellas expand, and glamour girls, undressed down to a G-string, gaze through their bejewelled sunglasses, after the water-skiers whizzing behind the yachts –, there the twitter of those in the purple patch and here the moaning of the damned. In a land whose thoughts will be protected by lead mines and casemates, whose thoughts are revealed by means of subcutaneous injections, other mechanisms for draining ideas are at work than in those regions where the psychologists meet at spas and the philosophers gather for feasts so decorative that the floriculturists are delighted. A kind of stagnating consciousness will be at work here, blunt and idle, bent over on itself under gusts from Nirvana.

A brain, that finds this stance neither tormenting nor insane, may be capable of stirrings that will take it to those spheres, those shuttlecock spheres, in which the lightest net decides the balls' direction, – to the badminton game of things. Streams of lemon-coloured silk, of apple-coloured silk, of cucumber-coloured silk, or the fawn throw rug that wraps the knees of the Secretary of State on his car rides in northern and in wind-swept lands during the leafy month of June, or white hyacinths and lilies of the valley in bloom are not the only ones to salvage the capacity to feel. From things within one's reach, too, even from handiwork, honey may drip into the spoon of such a brain.

Sitting on the fence and gaining impressions of the Earth at rest, pulling its elements apart, and once again, putting them together – the principle of those active on Olympus and of the Mahdis, and of the Norns, as well – add to this the sense of transformation at work in older peoples that intermingled with us, – the ideational method of tat twam asi: the lowering into things, and then the renewal in a grasp, in a flash, after the agony of the disproportionate confusion – all this only takes a step in the Ptolemaic landscape. It takes those enthralling hours, so rich, because it is neither work, the burden on the shoulders, nor the oars of the galleys that wear us out, make us so tired, but life as such, this fatalistic frame of mind, heavy and muddy, that brings us so close to the unbearable, and which we can repay in kind only an hour at a time. Nevertheless, from these generalities I now return to the flow of my personal notes, because with their help, I still aspire to continue on the way to a definite topic.

One must reckon with one thing for sure, there is no halting on this way, it is either everything or nothing, – the universe in the void. The human too can be brought under scrutiny only artistically, because this is certainly the way to the aesthetic world. This way is not cut for the possibility of lying: it rests on the certainty of the body and the nebulousness of the mind, that varies in its materializations. This way has got reality, that is to say, it lacks the finish, the swindle with the overpadded substitutes for natural substances, I speak about our continent and its renovators who write everywhere that the secret of its reconstruction lies in 'a deep, internal transformation of the principle of human personality' – not a morning without this whining in print! –, but wherever shoots of this transformation come to light, their systematic uprooting begins: prying in past and private lives, denunciations on account of State security, threat to the West, sabotage on humanity, – denunciation as a form of revolution, this whole, by now classic, method of the ideology of bigwigs, morons, and diploma holders; comparatively, scholasticism looks ultramodern and the witch trials as universal history. Now let us set that aside, it is outside my field; I throw myself into the arms of the future, though it hardly touches me either; detached, I watched the man-made rainfall, the result of cloud

38

tickling, the Squire-Kraus process – 150 pounds of dry ice on the cumulus formations; – the 200-inch telescope on Palomar Mount may register another twelve extragalactic nebulae; – Greenwich moves house to Tahiti and the Artic airbases communicate by means of transmitters the size of lipsticks, – and they are right not only because Napoleon said the last are always right, but rather because they are factually right within their sphere.

No, only the glance remains, the style, to see. Optimism –pessimism –: that presupposes the presence of opposites as fact or the wish to be someone in particular. Far off! There some Navy-Cut slips from a Russia-leather pouch, and there, a lime drop with a leaf of betel rolls out of a jade box. Admittedly, there are standpoints and visions before which the whole world collapses, paralytic visions, but they are not mine. I am no optimist, apart from the optimism of the businessman in whose till something rolls every day, – none at all, my entire life, and when one grows old, the great freeze begins, the retreat over the Berezina, the army defeated, the flag lowered, certain tattered bearskin caps managed as far as Poland, only the Emperor reached Paris, and I in my situation am no emperor. Of course there are also gratifying aspects, the birth of concepts, for instance, such as the *Rhizosphere*, I have just learnt of it today, it is the uppermost layer of humus within which the fauna is classified into edaphic, hemiedaphic, euedaphic and so on, according to its position in the depth of the soil; to the most recent layer belong mainly the springtails and the jerboa mice, that opens up gradually the 'animal world of the damp soils'. And where did all originate? Not in the damp soil, nor in the prints in the humus, no, but from a foothold in the open space, from predermination, and that is indeed my doctrine: man's unsusceptibility to experience. One needs to get rid of one's rigidity, put one's foot forward a little and stand there at ease, and as soon, the chest heaves differently. While there, quite a few things weigh on me, in any case, for instance: minus times minus equals plus – how come that minus times minus is the same as plus, what does that mean, who hit on that idea, whom did this lunacy hit all of a sudden in the face, that is neither logic nor psychology, neither causality nor calculation, that is of course an integral part of mathematics, but still pure phantasmagoria, and other-wordly game, to be grasped only as an isolated expression of itself. Thus here too, the traits of my type that never surrenders, always an introvert, breathing these gusts from Nirvana.

Pessimism, that is a convoluted thing -, but what does pessimism mean when everything is so clearly displayed? Downfall, - a people on the way to destruction, Sparta in the past, the Sioux as future, they will spend the next hundred years in single file, with incantations and some firewater from the rising victors. Downfall - down there one may carry on its kind of game quite happily, let its clouds move, adorn the windows with garlands, and from the windows once more greet the whole West imposant in its multifariousness and its profundity. They have got specialists for everything, for galaxies, and for Swahili dialects, and for sharks -, I have learnt that sharks are caught by pulling them by their tails so the water flows into their gills and that forces them to surface.

Pessimism - that is the roofed wickerwork beach chair of the unproductive type who drags it to the lake; I am an artist, I am interested in the counter-currents, prisms are my expertise, I work with glasses. What my method of writing down my observations, for instance, amounts to is prismatic infantilism, as it may be easily ascertained. It wakens memories of childhood games in everyone, we were running about with little pocket mirrors, trying to catch the sun in them which then we flashed upon the shopkeepers in front of their shops across the street. That aroused anger and bad blood, but we were under cover, in the shade. What we were bringing to light was naturally just skin, stucco, spots, moles of the outside, warts on the Olympus of appearances, nothing essential - that is why I will fold my hands before everyone who would rather read historical novels and see entire cultural eras spread before him, and wish him many sons to light his smoking pipe, to place before him bird's-nest soup with bêche-de-mer and turtle eggs, and together play fan-tan or mah-jong till the end of their days.

Nevertheless, there are glances and standpoints in which the worlds come together: the delirium about reclamation, the rock with the splinter, the jungle with the stone garden -, Gretchen walks towards Lachesis, the Epiphany talks to the last hours of summer, and Bonaparte's mausoleum sinks silently next to a mass grave. The Ptolemaic Earth and the slowly revolving Heaven, the repose and the colour of bronze under the soundless blue. Now and then, in spite of nevermore, instant and duration in one –, the maxim of the glass-blower, the lotus song, it sings of its hopes and its forgetting. No, I am no pessimist – where I come from, where I shall drop, I have got over all that. I spin a disk and am spun, I am a Ptolemaist. I do not groan as Jeremiah, I do not groan as Paul: 'I do not do what I like, only what I hate I do,' – I am the man I shall be, I do what strikes me. Nor do I carry any knowledge about my 'dereliction' as the modern philosophers: I have not been discarded, my birth has determined me. I am not made of 'existential anxiety', nor do I burden myself with wife and children, summer cottages and white ties; I wear discreet ties and my suit is impeccably cut, an earl on the outside and a pariah on the inside, mean, tough, impervious, let them eat whatever meat they come upon.

To come to terms with yourself, and occasionally cast an eye over the water. Mechanical gestures, lotions, customer service for the sake of the psychophysical ideal, – quite in top form: a widely-travelled and self-made hairdresser. The lessons of life, and then, at certain hours, this continent's last dream. The vultures and the water lilies, the business and the hallucinations, intersections and then the demise – that is how I stick out before the ascending lands.

I bring with me the fragility and the keenness of Nefertiti and besides, a multitude of memories from miraculously self-contained vaults: the Latinity and Christianity gathered by this continent into sums total and universals and by it dispersed. Traditions from Cordoba and Montpellier, gifts from apostles, troubadours and monks, germs of suffering and thoughts, enslavements to mechanisms and idols, experiments, decipherings of cuneiform writings, theses and statistics – inside the quantitatively determined human scale, a heavy brain, a loaded Pathétique.

'Lotus' – who inherits my business is not my concern; whether I shall be remembered it's beyond my space. From foreign papers I learn that one firm alone offers 67 brands of hairlotions and cosmetic preparations, so that trade is not dying, but when it is all over, they will find something else, oil for robots or salve for corpses – everything is as it will be, and the end is good.

THE RADAR THINKER

Autumn, – the season of asters and big spiders. Every morning one of these giants is sitting on the wall or in one of the washbasins: they cannot come through door panels nor climb out of water pipes, so wherefrom do they land here, I am asking myself every September, now I am going to look it up, the zoologists should know.

Quite often in the morning I sit on a special wooden stool by the window overlooking the street. Now and then I allow myself to do just that. To travel, I cannot, because of the expenses and difficulties which such an enterprise entails, and on the other hand, I haven't received a passport to enable me to go out of the city. I am on all the black lists, black sheep – reason: I do not think about many things as most people do. At the same time I often form a mental image of the members of parliaments, they can talk and write anything, they are immune inside the parliament building as much as in the street, nobody dares to be hard on them, everybody must support them; only when they are caught red-handed are they brought to book. Furthermore, some of them say quite extreme things, dangerous to the State, and hostile to the public, so what they say is either considered humbug and they are not taken seriously or it is an injustice committed against the words of the Psalmist: righteousness elevates a people to honour.

The sitting is pleasant – not as if I were unsure of my movements. The crippled restaurateur across the street from me, abuse of alcohol, old syphilis, the right eyelid no longer goes up, but damaged in other ways, too, he is unable to walk properly, yet keeps daydreaming cheerfully in the front garden of his establishment, and spinning to himself. What he is brooding upon, what yarn he is telling himself, I wonder, and wonder time and again.

Here is a capital question. It may be the following: a man is elected head of State, the so-called President, an extremely likeable man, without a flaw, his electoral victory had been unexpected, yet only 48 hours later, a delegation made up of girls in traditional dress, hailing from his very remote hometown, showed up and presented him with a flower garland and a basketful of grapes. When you come to think of it: the news of his victory spread home, and hastily a committee is set up, which seizes upon this idea, finds the girls, rigs them out, gives them money, they must be put on the train, instructed, they must arrive and be welcomed - all this within 48 hours! What a wonderful human spirit of enterprise, what activity, effervescence, what progress in timing and publicity - who could keep up with it! Here the ball is passed from one to the other, and decision and execution become perfect right away and all round.

The likes of us look everywhere for connections but find none, one spends one's life hunting for particulars. But connections do exist, naive, experienced. A day in summer, Sunday, you walk along the Commercial Street, saunter into a coffee shop, it's full, find a chair by the wall, a table for two, a man is already sitting there, an apparition! Says abruptly: in the last 6 months the city has changed drastically. So a conversation is set off. A stranger, an old Jew, completely deaf, hearing aids in the auditory canals, uncommonly likeable! Then he brings in his children, the daughter-in-law - You raise from the table half an hour later having learnt the following: most of his life He has been travelling in Southern Germany, headquarters in Stuttgart, son is editor, lives in low-rent housing, view from the hill - son-in-law doctor in the SS, stupid boy, sentenced to twenty-two years, remitted, not yet denazified, today (Sunday), in Sommerheim am Wasser, surgeon, orthopedics, Thursday afternoons free, but too tired - he, the narrator, in very poor health, inguinal hernia, scrotal hernia, hangs out, doesn't retract, must wear a hernial bandage, put it on, take it off, mornings and evening in bed, to avoid any accident, in addition, cardiac insufficiency, advanced arteriosclerosis, does not dare to smoke in earnest, but today is Sunday, nobody sees him here -, stone-deaf, impossible to answer him, he alone talks, but uncommonly likeable, humanly frank and communicative (a goy would have sat there dull and dumb, rude, self-righteous) - this one here is articulate, expansive, youth and age together, spaces intertwine: petrol in Stuttgart is 60 pfennings, in Frankfurt 90, at Marienborn I bought another hundred litres for 1.20 DM, idiotic, here in the East, 50 pfennings -- briefly a bunch of blooming facts, no gaps, no grief, life fulfilled!

On another occasion, you sit in a bar on a roof terrace, you go seldom out, everything makes a strong impression on you, the white napkins, the clean waiters, well groomed couples – but why do people dance jerking, zigzagging, perspire and the sweat is running down on them, and plasters the hair on their heads – they move rhythmically, run here to there, pleasure-seeking, swinging, gyrating full of passion, small dance floor in front of the band – erotism or snuggling up or a class of slimming, anyway they are at it in earnest, and somewhat the confined space keeps them together. Here, too, something universal, something good becomes apparent.

The days of summer, however, are gone, as already said. The hours fly like sparks, autumn, this faltering, it stirs so! Faltering, why hesitate and conceal what soon will become obvious: the cold skies and the night, the separation, after which the years and the days have torn our hearts to shreds with lunacies and forgetfulness, and the distant, clear peals that start all of a sudden. The man at the window! The trains of thought at home! The radar thinker in his armchair! But the causality has only shifted towards the outside in the last few centuries; cause and effect and the reaction deriving from that, but strictly speaking, nothing of the kind. Causality lies in yourself, you rule over matter: Stockholm is a glaring city, parks and walls of houses ablaze with explosions, and in other parts of the Earth you chance on regions that smell of fragrant sumac, and others, of violets. The outer causality brings nothing nearer. You must always go out and look for something, the inner causality enriches you as you sit in your chair – Siam, that land sunken in lotus flowers, where an eternal Saturday afternoon reigns, the realm which has always had fish in its waters and rice in its paddies! Or in philology: spiritual states, two thousand years old, empty phrases of humility, formulae of self-disparagement ('my feeble talent', 'quacking in my shoes', 'my rambling speech'), so-called topoi, literary constants, rhetorical dedicatory phrases going back to the ancients – Cicero! – there you see deep, deep behind the ruins of civilization, the silenced forms of being will regain their exuberance in you -- do you know the Processional Way? Right and left the lions of golden enamel, in the distance the Gate of Ishtar – a play of glaze and multicoloured bricks – 120 lions! – you see them along the walls there –: there, perspective!

In all earnestness, examine the situation! You sit here in your chair and outside begins the onslaught upon the Tropics. West Africa in the foreground, but Nigeria, too. There where

800,000 people lived so far, now 10 billion will be fed – an afflux! But who hastens towards it – you, perchance? Eventful surroundings! The New South Wales has had the coldest day in 79 years – snow in Canberra; short-lived army revolt in Honduras! And you? You know the change in the order of the day that passes over without further ado. The Indian zoos are presented with a giant salamander as a token of friendship by Japan, there is hope that science will be able eventually to save the eyes attainted by flukes – and you? Let us say it quietly: we only exist as traces!

What is all this for, where is the core? What do we know about people? The trio from Der Rosenkavalier – wherefrom does it derive its charm, the overture to Traviata, or the spirituals, the songs of the slaves –, why do they move us to tears? All is unclear. Nonetheless, man's nature has been discussed a lot, really, without respite, for the last two thousand years. There have been very many crises, as well, some consider the decline of the Roman Empire as the most drastic crisis, others think so of the present. To me, crisis is too casual a word. You think you are ahunting whereas you are hunted – demons, scaly saurians, glacial periods, oscillations of the axis of the Earth, organ reshapings – a long series of oddities, incomprehensible to the domesticated problematizer of floor and garden allotment issues. Still, whoever has got his training by radar methods has it easy, places a piece of cardboard on his desk on which is written in large letters: There is nothing else.

Conflicts are not excluded, of course. You are limp and covered with sores, so you don't answer the telephone and dread the postman – and then a lady comes to you, who could not eat to her heart's desire the previous evening because of the prescription pills. Her son celebrated his jubilee, twenty-five years of practice as orthopedic surgeon, four other friends were there, two of them doctors, as well, they always make music together, her son plays all the instruments, but violin in particular, wonderful food, but she could not do it justice. Then she goes on to speak of her daughter, another jubilee, she sings and plays the harmonium at memorial services – another jubilee – life can be so simple: tablets, loss of apetite and jubilee – nothing about sores!

Nothing about dialectics – the silhouettes move gradually. They move along the pavement. The female half, women, no ladies, nor have they got any money, but they raise their heads, hold themselves erect, the men look at them from behind, they feel it on their hips, and those men, all incriminated one way or another, miserably deflated politically, without a situation but managing somehow, they sleep during the night, then they wake up in the morning basically in high spirits – always this getting up, to join in, to carry on till Easter as they do now, at the end of autumn – well, and, just a moment, there comes a lady with a hat on, good heavens, were she to stand still, an excited crowd would gather in no time: gillyflowers of all colours, taut, and on top of them, a tuft with an independent existence, amidst the lushness of details that compose the joke – that is the calm before the storm: if this fashion catches on, Melanesia and Timbuktu will sway along my street!

Of course there are hours of uncertainty, as well, against that one feels the need of a monument like that of Storm, medium-size block of granite, a bust with black coat and beard, heather wreaths on the plinth – the beautiful Immensee, played softly, but still audible – meadows all round – all these Elizabethan poems by many authors – but one must bear it.

If now someone says that what the man at the window does is not unlike what is going on aboard a fishing boat catching herring, sonar and vibration detector, but only for the lower depths, yet I can also point out that such extraordinary things may be found in newspapers and the like, as well. A diplomat from the safest country in the world, no German, internationally known by the high offices he has held, in a testimonial writes the following: 'The clearest symptoms of the complete and catastrophic transformation of the times had already reached the last stage in which all of a sudden all names, all words had lost their meaning, the signs and symbols which the intellect had created in architecture as in musical composition are no longer true, everything lies, everything fades out, only to become extinct all of a sudden and disappear completely.'

Monstrous words! It is a diplomat who takes the soundings here! One from an eminent family of the old style, the best in Europe as hierarchy goes, and as good manners on the golf course, testifies in detail about the last stage of our era in his quality of expert.

Thus the era frizzles up, somewhere something goes up in

flames, and somewhere something is put out and sinks into the ashes of the worlds; somewhere a nova, and somewhere a shadow, and somewhere a water glass in which the serum stirs itself. At first the five books of Genesis, and then the instant when life is experienced only in the brain, the innards become insensible, yet awareness grows more aware. Firstly the Genesis, and then the fifth angel with his trumpet, in those days people will seek death but will not find it, because the locusts, come out of the smoke, have been told that they were not to kill but rather torment.

They succeeded in their torments! Torment by ideas, torment by abolition of ideas –: Have you not made it clear to yourself once for all that almost everything that today's mankind still thinks, calls thinking, can by this time be thought by machines made by cybernetics, the new science of creation? And these machines outdo even man, the valves are more precise, the circuits more stable than in our distressed wreck, they process letters into sounds and provide 8 hours of memory; sick parts may be extirpated and replaced by new ones. So thinking goes into the robot which satisfies the need, the rest are rudiments of a volcanic time gone by, and wherever they show up, they already look inhuman and bankrupt. So where do you stand, at what point of the fauna, through what flora do your feet still shove – you rake through the autumnal dream, the roses bend over their tumbler – empty, a last trickle on the wallpaper, the gardens wisper brown and purple, blending with the flat country in the distance.

What I speak of here is not the outside, the inner gaze though is steady and deep. First of all: admittedly the creator had wanted to bring forth and develop something in the way of goodness and forgiveness in man, it must also be admitted that he wanted to develop something murderous and blood-thirsty in tigers and leopards, and to that it must be added as well that by and large he has been successful. The substances which should evince those parts in man that are connected with his superiority are not so simple, all the more so, given that the creator has succeeded only meagrely and sporadically in that regard. To sum up: can it be assumed at all that the creator strove for the human form, no, there is no doubt that it cannot. Secondly: you learn, or more likely, you are handed down from tradition, thesauri, ancestral lumber, that God helps those who help themselves; or Goethe, so much celebrated: defiantly to withstand all powers is to summon the gods to one's aid - or Dehmel: 'Help yourself, then eat and suffer,' - or Hebbel: 'To the striplings' - or as the in-depth psychology has it: 'Only by heeding his possibilities can man rise to his true self' - in short, an abundance of popular, scientific, aesthetic opinions, verses, maxims, all telling you that you must keep yourself under control, find your own voice, persevere - all taught in school, belonging to the universal, and now as a young, educated man, you find yourself face to face with these truths - should you, do you have the courage to reject everything, do you have the courage, should you cram religion into the cupboard, contrary to what grows naturally, to popular wisdom? Thirdly: I have been observing myself very closely, I can do that, because I think of myself as so unimportant. In middle age, I did not return the affection of someone special, nothing erotic, rather something of an intimate relationship, I made him suffer, held him at arm's length, turned him away from me, he was weak, suffered, and lastly, he died. As a result I set about observing myself to see whether it did me any harm. I have continued these introspections relentlessly to this day, they brought up dark thoughts and still more sorrow, but no collapse, in any case, I have not been able to notice any obvious harm to my life. Likewise, I have allowed letters, announcements, requests to go unanswered, that is, I simply turned a deaf ear to human communicativeness, those things bored me, there was no stimulus in them. In other words, all that did not come out as morally as it should, so at times, I still believe that life has got no other meaning but that every twenty-four hours one grows older by a day, one sleeps at night, and in the morning, between ten and eleven, the beard grows longer - oh, at times I believe that even the brave witnesses and the good minders feel that their positions have long been untenable.

And awareness grows more aware, the second week of the creation begins, but when evening descends upon the garden, see, it is no good. Cold and grief! If the saying goes that nature has got the traits of the jungle, how much more impenetrable is the mind and its movements. It is not what the public understands by it. There where it emerges truly into the open, it tells nothing, makes no small talk; there, by way of example, it pulls out man's brain convolutions directly, piecemeal, grey matter, and in no way restores them but rather

51

continues the destruction. Opaque procedure: it strikes the right notes but their reverberation is out of tune, it takes one direction out which ultimately proves to be barren, as it runs forth, sprawls headlong and sinks. You feel the objections to it, to yourself, but it chases you on, it burns its fire, yet it strews even its own ashes quite by itself. These days it converts itself usually into opinions. An opinion takes the bite, a shiver runs through its body, the teeth grind, it shakes the stuff, tears it up – shreds and dust! Opinions get into a muddle like the lizards in the sunshine – now they must be big ideas. Crocodiles, aground, but I miss the writ about the domestic character of the axiom and the geography of the apriori, the climatic justification for so much dust! These days, it would be taken for entertainment, science, propaedeutic – oh, dear God – *these days! These days* you may find yourself in the situation in which you are asked what do you live on, you cannot live on radar opinions. Formerly there were fine positions – company lawyer: smart contracts, new emissions, or otolaryngologist: a little jab on the pharynx and no night calls. – Salesman for Suchard chocolate, much in demand, you only have to lift the receiver and make a note of the order – especially when you examine the notion of work, you come to strange results, but they were beautiful times and I cherish their memory. *These days* there is the rage the world over that everything must be kept warm: soles, truths, colours – leg warmers – thermals, that is the background – thermals as pennant for the kamikaze, the divine wind, the death flier – thermals round the pikes of the apocalyptic riders – they want ground under their feet 'again' (as if they had it anywhere for 500 years), 'Back to the classics, so we've gone no farther' (farther, but whereto then, and what does 'so' mean?) – 'Humus' – thus quietly they want muck on the boots – but warm muck –– personally I do not believe in restoration, the spiritual things are irreversible, they go on to the end, to the end of the night. *These days, these days* – but publicly I make allowances for that, I always say, these days we are in Egypt, so make your way quietly in the direction of the information bureaux and counters, but keep your head free, in it there must always be some empty space for creation. Here is the real which concentrates, moulds itself, and so creates the forms. You do not need to look at the watch – ¼ to six or ¼ to seven – phantoms, all! But we don't want to be too strict either, think of man's life, it squeezes itself through the day, grows thinner, grows thicker, carries tufts of chamois hair, puts up with pleuresy, dotes on perineal tears, stuffs ear holes, and then all too quickly comes the hour when it must stick its face into the dark, into the great black sponge, and ultimately they all have gone on the pilgrimage and from the look on the face they grasp that very soon they will have to leave, and the hubbub of voices in railway stations, where nobody is of any use to them.

Streets stream through millions of towns, during the day a lake on the left side, a blue of the creation, and nights, the neon lights. Riverbridge, Ponte Vecchio, Münsterbrücke – beyond them, the strange, the distant, not erected by you, not built for you. The peripheries of the metropolis: giant structures or Père Lachaise or pineapple plantations – but strangers, nonetheless, those who walk through the fields. The lips of children, the age of the Earth, but you cannot take all that in. The year 1821 Shelley drowned between Leghorn and Lerici – long ago, Voltaire lived in a manor house – long past. Sorrow from all the distances psychically afflicts the ages, melancholy from a long perspective. That is why I teach little things – do you busy yourself with little things quietly at your window: shun the distant, shun the duration, do not look so far, whenever you look in the distance, you know, of course, the question will always pop up: if none of these would have happened, the splitting of the atom, dynamite, insulin, edible lupin – what then, what would it all have looked like to you then, but first, supposedly something else would have happened, or secondly, nothing else would have happened, yet does it change the premisses of the world in any way? No, shun the distant, entwine yourself with your inner possessions, remove your pictures from the walls, be Alcibiades or Helen or Ephialtes, betray, otherwise you will be betrayed, or both, to be sure --, the heartbreaking, always the heartbreaking, there you are, and you must live with it. The backward glance, just as well: three years, what immense a time span, three years free of incarceration or prostate carcinoma, what aeon-long gift from the higher authorities, believe me, there is nothing more, there is nothing more to be granted, it is already a respite from the descent and the end of the inexplicable meaning which the gods may be quick to punish! Stand up, feast your eyes on each twilight, end the day the way the boss leaves his office: 'Anything else?'

Convince yourself, it has been thought through, no more records to break! Look at the wedding announcements, everything in them still breathes spiritual refinement and elegance. The animals spread themselves in all directions, but man is at the end of his tether, by and large, there is very little about him in what he says. We are dumb, we are unfit, we are not the favourites, you already tremble in front of your typewriter, you strike the keys, empty, hollow sockets, something quite dry, and then you set something together - a word oozing of dreams and mist, spontaneously a while, solemnly bringing closer something from the other side, and clearly, something from this side - hybrid world, intermixtures - who is there to show you the way? The man with a house of his own! To look from the shade out, onto the luminous trees and flowers - the Japanese garden principle - its window invites you to do it. To keep yourself in the shade, to linger - the world comes to a halt!

Now come the industrious and say, your shadows are dumb, we want instead to neigh and warble, be *natural*, your shadows are empty - but that is just it: there is no emptiness and there is no fullness, there is only the possibility, to fill the emptiness here, without delay, at the window, by casting the plumbline and by transformation. Then come the young and say, we cannot live like that, we want stuff, we want skills, we want ideals - we want, we want, we want --: so they want coupling and immortality, but what does it look like? An immortality of 50 years, not even the lifespan of a tortoise, with the help of auctions, mementos, new neighing, new warbling - 50 years - what metaphysical frugality, what unpretentious will to live - no, it does not satisfy me, I want to be dead, fully, ashes, worm, earth, weeds, I bend my head and take myself with me - once for all, I would not put up with another life, nor can it be - only once in the turmoil of dreams and images.

This thesis of man puts up with aeons. To outgrow tensions, to tie up tensions - to reconcile, that is the secret of style! What you call crisis does not stop you from gaining weight; look round you, crisis - that is but the good, old tradition, here and there, charming play of opposites: under tyrants freedom hardens, and under pious emperors, the life of pleasures - hear another tune from the big trumpet, a word, harsh but comforting: *fate!* Mind and life – what was that, after all? Let us recall, my friends, the 2nd of December 1942, as the vibrating needles of the measuring instruments started to move, small nuggets of uranium, containing enriched uranium 235, were piled up like bricks, on top of one another, in the squash court in the basement of the sports arena of the University of Chicago, while the unsuspecting pedestrians were walking on the pavement above – so it reached the point when the instruments went buzzing, but Fermi, the imperturbable leader and inaugurator of the neutron bombardment, the new creator with a grasp of the celebration and the light and of the separation of waters, caretaker of the Second Genesis, uttered the famous words: 'Let us have something to eat first.'

II

The preceding emanations were meant to convey a state of mind for which there is no objective explanation and no individual justification. The brain is round, soft, capable of expanding – its function is to convert into actuality. The radar thinker had to develop his faculties, he had to express in words what his reality was in those autumn days. Now we must observe him from the outside, and that yields the following:

I imagine a dialogue, what was the name of your lady friend of 20 years ago? Ellen Lohmeyer. What did she look like? Like all women, medium size, mop of hair on top. How did you get on? As one does, half lust and half boredom. What was the parting like? We split up – *Mind you*: things happen like that, even those loaded with reality, even the genuine. For the radar thinker there is nothing more to it, indeed – Ellen Lohmeyer – a somewhat universal currency with tokens from those in position.

One must in all earnest raise some objections against a passage in his monologue. The finality which planes over his being, that is the genuine mood, the personal wave. You rummage through the autumn dream – I wish myself dead – that is the limitation of the sight, overaccentuation, apathy. On the other hand, it is his attempt to say everything in one sentence, to make it stand on its own, to round it off; there is no room, time and stopgaps for the introvert man in it, so the isolated sentences and paragraphs are set one next to the other with no thematic connection between them (typographically the juxtaposition is not possible) but to render them in blocks is fashionable. Nevertheless, he has not sufficiently considered an idea which we want to pursue because it is fundamental and almost cancels him out.

The matter is briefly as follows. The idea to which he had not given enough thought is that man is not an end, not the summit of creation, rather a beginning. What ails him, what depresses him, what dismays him are the diseases of childhood, teething disorders, growing pains – he is not yet put in position inside the new construction. In fact, a systematic boundary of the first order exists between the two species of anthropoids and sapiens on the one side, and the entire preceding world, on the other. Apes, mammals, vertebrates, on the whole the animal kingdom is surpassed, left behind; emancipated, the mind is groping for a newly opened space. Let us consider the beginning of the Deluge. Its representatives in China! The mastery of fire, the organization of the environment, the expansion of the environmental area by the technical means of the stone age. Nothing accidental! Most of the body-build was complete. The nerve fibres in the Precambrian; the internal skeleton in the Silurian; the stepping on firm land, that is walking feet, in the Upper Devonian; the zygomatic arch in the Permian; birthing in the Jurassic; in the Mesozoic, warm blood and so on – now begins the first ligature of Act II.

A leaf that drops from a tree, antlers, their lives follow a certain rhythm, but as they drop, their lives end. Now the immaterial things branch out, become transmissible, are passed on, and conserved. Starlings, mocking birds, parrots imitate the song of other species of birds, but now there begins the objectively consistent speech. Millions of years behind it – and now, for the first time, this short interval! The plasticity of becoming turns to new dimensions, openly concentrates all its powers upon this topic, varies in its unfoldings – no sign of exhaustion. The future is incalculable, but man probably will not come to an end. As ice ages, the floods, moon falls did not do him in, nor can the atomic bomb threaten him. Lamentations! The species conserve themselves and come to an end on other grounds, obviously, according to laws that are above the neutrons. We shall be, we are: old animistic rudiments and the

56

new technical reality. Each is included – nobody can be more than some universal currency with tokens from those in position. So Ellen Lohmeyer quite big – led to the table by genetics and palaeonthology, the overture begins, composed in ultrasounds, performed by conch players.

NOTES

PTOLEMY'S DISCIPLE: A BERLIN NOVELLA, 1947

Page 3: **Raskolnikov had killed**...: Allusion to the protagonist of the novel *Crime and Punishment* (1866) by the Russian writer Fyodor Dostoyevsky (1821–1881). Benn repeatedly referred to the moral dilemma in that novel, and in particular, in his poem 'St.Petersburg – Mid Century'(1943), ET in *Poems 1937–1947* (1991), pp.73–77.
Page 4: **and the loess**...: a reformulation of a Vedic principle – the pottery breaks but the clay remains.
Page 4: **the Mings**...: Chinese imperial dynasty (1368–1644).
Page 4: **Kepler or Galilei**...:Johannes Kepler(1571–1630), German astronomer and mathematician who established that the planets, the Earth included, revolved about the Sun in eliptical orbits; Galileo Galilei (1564–1642), Italian mathematician, astronomer and physicist, supporter of the Copernican theory of the solar system and developer of an astronomical telescope by means of which he discovered craters on the Moon and Jupiter's satelites, among other things, and showed that the Milky Way is composed of stars.
Page 4: **Rectification of Names**...: Famous doctrine of Confucius (c551–479BC), according to which degeneration of political and social systems, considered to start from the top, may give way to regeneration, that is, restoration of order by arranging affairs in such a manner as reality in each case should correspond to the names, in other words, the Emperor should continue to be Emperor, the nobles, noble, and so on ('Let the ruler be ruler, the minister, minister; let the father be father, and the son, son.')
Page 4: **era of mathematics**...: Apparrently throughout the novella, Benn used as source for his mathematical references the book *Geist der Mathematik* [The Spirit of Mathematics] by his friend Max Bense (1910–1990), first published in 1939.
Page 4: **Descartes–Pascal–Leibnitz**...:René Descartes(1596–1650), French philosopher, mathematician and physicist, inventor of analytical geometry, and among other things, of the methodological bases of modern science; Blaise Pascal (1623–1662), French mathematician, physicist, philosopher and writer, forerunner of the modern theory of probabilities; Gottfried Wilhelm Leibnitz (1646–1716), German philosopher, mathematician and logician, founder of calculus and of the dynamic theory of motion.
Page 4: **on Euclid by Proclus**...:Euclid (3rd c. BC), Greek mathematician, taught at Alexandria during the rule of Ptolemy I, author of several works among which a treatise on geometry, *The Elements*; Proclus(c410–485AD), Greek Neoplatonic philosopher, and also author of mathematical and astronomical works.
Page 4: **logic of Boole**...: George Boole (1815–1864), British mathematician and symbolic logician, whose algebra has been basic for the development of digital computers.
Page 5: **and Pierce, of Russell and Hilbert**...: Charles Sanders Pierce (1839–1914), American logician, philosopher and man of science, best known for his work on the logic of relations, and a promoter of pragmatism as method of research; Bertrand Russell (1872–1970), British mathematical logician and philosopher; David Hilbert (1862–1943), German mathematician with a strong interest in mathematical physics, worked on infinite-dimensional

58

space.

Page 5: with the name of Hume...:David Hume (1711-1776), Scottish philosopher and economist, who among other things, maintained that cause and effect are not observable features in objects but are inferred from their contiguity in space and succession in time, as well as from the constant conjunction of like objects in the past.

Page 7: a thriller by Edgar Wallace...:Edgar Wallace (1875-1932), prolific British author and journalist, best known for his detective stories or 'thrillers'.

Page 9: related how his daughter...: This is an indirect way of relating a personal experience - the first visit after the war his daughter, 'a war correspondent' under the British flag, paid him in Berlin. Before including it in the novella, Benn wrote about the incident to his Bremen friend, F.W. Oelze, in a letter of 14 April 1946. See *Briefe an F.W. Oelze, 1945-1949*, pp. 25-27.

Page 10: Nietzsche did in fact say...:Friedrich Nietzsche(1844-1900), German philosopher, classicist and psychologist. Benn refers to the last two paragraphs of the Second Chapter of Nietzsche's *Unmodern Observations*, entitled 'History in the Service and Disservice of Life', ET 1990, pp. 144-145.

Page 14: the antireticular cytotoxic serum...:Benn learnt about it, like about so many other things, from newspapers and periodicals, and in this particular case from an article published in *Die Neue Zeitung* of 7 February 1947, a discovery of a certain American, Dr Henry Goldblatt; Benn queries F.W. Oelze about it and other findings to be included in the novella, in a letter of 11 February 1947, op. cit., pp. 67-68.

Page 14: Aprèslude...: a play on words on the pattern of 'prelude', with an opposite meaning to it - it is not an introductory piece of music or verse but a coda. Eight years later, Benn will send his publisher a cycle of twenty-five poems with that title, which he also uses for one of the poems in it.

Page 14: for my friend O...: Reference to Dr Friedrich Wilhelm Oelze (1891-1978), Benn's great friend from Bremen and constant correspondent, to whom he entrusted clean copies of his MSS for preservation during the war years and after, and so avoid irretrievable loss; Dr Oelze never let him down. About Dr Oelze see Benn's *Double Life*, ET 2002, p. 140.

Page 15: from de Sitter...:Willem de Sitter (1872-1934), Dutch astronomer, best known for his work on relativity and the expansion of the universe.

Page 15: which Eckhart saw...: Johannes Eckhart, better known as Meister Eckhart (c1260-c1327), German Dominican speculative mystic, author of *The Treatises* (four in number) and other works, and whose originality resides in the personal mystical experience that served as basis for his sermons and philosophy.

Page 15: winks to Ananke...: Ananke is the personification of fate or necessity in post-Homeric Greek literature and theology.

Page 15: new Athoses and new Monte Cassinos...: Mount Athos represents the agglomeration of Orthodox Christian monasteries on the northernmost finger of the Chalcidice Peninsula, jutting into the Aegean Sea, in North-Eastern Greece, dating from the 10th century and forming a unique theocratic State; Monte Cassino was a famous Benedictine abbey, situated between Rome and Naples and founded by St Benedict in 529AD. It was destroyed during WWII but was rebuilt afterwards.

Page 16: silent tat twam asi...: Vedic Brahman formula, translated into English as 'Thou Art That', which points to the identity of essence - you should be aware of the identity of your innermost essence with the invisible substance of all and everything.

Page 17: **A famous writer**...:Reference to André Gide (1869-1951), the French writer and to an article of his, printed in *Die Neue Zeitung* of 7 February 1947.

Page 18: **second thermodynamic law of the existential**...: Ironic associative reference to the second law of thermodynamics, dealing with thermal energy (heat) and stating that heat flows from a higher to a lower temperature but not the other way round.

Page 18: **Li Hung-chang had**...:Li Hung-chang(1823-1901), Chinese statesman who spent long years in Europe and negotiated China's reconciliation with the Western Powers in 1901.

Page 18: **Isvolski must have**...: Alexandr Petrovich Isvolski (1856-1919), Russian diplomat and foreign minister (1906-1910), then the Tsar's ambassador in Paris (1910-1917), where he died two years later.

Page 18: **Then Caruso**...: Enrico Caruso (1873-1921), Italian tenor, most famous operatic singer of early 20th century, and the first to be recorded on discs, made his Metropolitan Opera debut in 1903, becoming its quasi permanent asset for the rest of his life.

Page 18: **Gatti-Casazza, the administrator**...:Giulio Gatti-Casazza (1869-1940), Italian impressario, became the sole general manager of the Metropolitan Opera in New York between 1910 and 1935.

Page 19: **at a thinking genius' place**...: Reference to Friedrich Nietzsche's living conditions.

Page 20: **what Bülow recorded**...:Bernhard von Bülow (1849-1929), German foreign state secretary, imperial chancellor and Prussian prime minister, describes his first visit to the estate of former German chancellor Otto von Bismarck (1815-1898) in the first volume of his *Memoirs*, ET 1931, p. 27.

Page 21: **such as Tegel, or upon the house of Goethe**...: Reference to the castle on the Lake Tegel, in the northern part of Greater Berlin, which was the residence of Wilhelm von Humboldt (1767-1835), Prussian education minister, linguist, diplomat, man of letters and thinker, friend of Schiller and Goethe; Johann Wolfgang von Goethe (1749-1832), German writer, and Weimar courtier for the greater part of his life, was presented by his patron Duke Carl August with a handsome Italianate house in the middle of Weimar, that eventually became a museum.

Page 22: **the great old soloist**...: Allusion to Bismarck, see above note for page 20.

Page 22: **Kitchener sticks**...: Horatio Herbert Kitchener (1850-1916), British field marshal, conqueror of the Sudan, following the battle of Omdurman in 1898, commander in chief during the Anglo-Boer War, and eventually secretary of state for war at the beginning of WWI.

Page 22: **Gordon is avenged**...:Charles George Gordon (1833-1885), British general, who by his exploits in China in 1869, and his ill-fated defence of Khartoum against Sudanese rebels in 1885, gained the posthumous fame of national hero and martyr.

Page 22: **where Moltke waves**...:Helmuth von Moltke (1800-1891), Chief of the Prussian and the German General Staffs, main strategist of the German victories over Denmark, Austria and France.

Page 23: **Discern the situation**...: The first five maxims are first mentioned by Benn in a letter to Dr Oelze of 2 October 1936, in which he expresses his opinion about the Swedish writer and playwright August Strindberg (1849-1912). See *Briefe an FW Oelze, 1932-1945*, pp.149-150. 'Erkenne die Lage' (Discern the situation) or as it has also been translated, 'take stock of the situation' is a fundamental existential and juridical principle for periods of transition, and an imperative of clinical medicine. Benn adopted it together with the others for his own use and for the benefit of his readers;

his personal contribution is item No. 6, the use of sedatives to keep oneself under control. (Benn had suffered of atrocious headaches all his life, accompanied by a high degree of tension and irritability, precursory symptoms of what was to become his terminal cancer of the spine.)

Page 26: **Om mani padme hum**...: a Vedic mantra, or sacred utterance possessing spiritual efficacy, that has been turned into a purely mechanical means to obtain wordly and spiritual ends, most widespread in Tibet.

Page 31: **ora et labora**...: Latin phrase meaning 'prayer and toil'.

Page 32: **songs about Tamerlane**...:Also known as Timur Lenk (c1336–1405), a Turkic conqueror of the Islamic faith from Central Asia.

Page 34: **GROWTH OF THE SOIL and THE RAINS CAME**...:The former is a novel by the Norwegian writer and Nobel Prize winner Knut Hamsun (1859–1952), originally published in 1917, ET in 1920; the latter is the 1937 novel by the American writer Louis Bromfield (1896–1956).

Page 35: **panta rhei**...:Greek phrase, meaning 'all flows' or 'all is in flux'.

Page 35: **Kublai Khan moves**...:Kublai Khan (1214–1294), Mongolian Emperor of China (1260–1294), grandson of Genghis Khan, completed the conquest of the Chinese territories, but showed tolerance in religious matters.

Page 35: **grandfather Genghis Khan turns**...:Temudjin Genghis Khan (c1160–1227), founder of the first Mongol Empire, conquered Northern China in 1215, after which he advanced westwards into Europe and southwards into Afghanistan.

Page 35: **which Clive gave**...: Robert Clive, Baron Clive of Plassey (1725–1774), British general, established the British administrative authority in India.

Page 36: **the Yuan dynasts**...:Established by Kublai Khan as the first Mongol dynasty, they ruled China between 1279 and 1368. Although under their rule, China became a vast empire with extensive foreign trade and outstanding achievements in public works, civil engineering and culture, their incomplete sinicization and their use of foreigners in administration made of them the shortest–lived dynasty in the history of Imperial China.

Page 36: **the Merovingians would**...: The first royal dynasty of the Franks, centred in Gaul (476–751AD), overthrown by the Carolingians.

Page 36: **if one lets Hans Sachs out**...:Hans Sachs (1494–1576), German poet and songwriter, had been apprenticed to a shoemaker and became a master cobbler in 1519, trade which he practised throughout his life alongside his poetry.

Page 36: **Spinoza in any case**...:Benedict Spinoza (1632–1677), Dutch independent rationalist and religious thinker, excommunicated by the local Jewish authorities for his non–orthodox biblical exegesis in 1656, earned his living by grinding and polishing lenses. The Olympian who admired his thinking was Goethe, the German poet and author.

Page 41: **I do not groan as Paul**...: See Apostle Paul's Letters to the Romans, 7,15.

THE RADAR THINKER

Page 45: **righteousness elevates**...: See Proverbs, 14,34.

Page 47: **– Cicero! –**...:Marcus Tullius Cicero (106BC–43AD), Roman lawyer, statesman, scholar and orator, who in his qualities of senator and barrister, raised rhetoric to unprecedented heights in Roman culture, only ultimately to do him in.

Page 47: **the Processional Way?**...:Street in ancient Babylon, leading from the Ishtar Gate to the great temple of Esagila.

Page 48: **from Der Rosenkavalier**...: Or *The Knight of the Rose*, opera in three acts by the German composer Richard Strauss with a libretto by the

Austrian poet Hugo von Hofmannsthal, first performed in 1911.

Page 48: **overture to Traviata**...:The various editors of Benn's collected works have consistently opted for a different title, that is, 'Violetta', ignoring Benn's own correction. *La Traviata* is an Italian opera in three acts by Giuseppe Verdi (1813-1901), first performed in 1853.

Page 49: **like that of Storm**...:Hans Storm (1817-1888), German poet, novelist and lawyer, was an outstanding representative of poetic realism; *Immensee*, an early novel of his (1852, ET 1863) is a moving and nostalgic story of vanished childhood.

Page 49: **It is a diplomat**...:Identified as Carl Jacob Burckhardt (1891-1974), Swiss diplomat, formerly League of Nations Commissioner for Danzig, was a witness at the War Criminals' Trials at Nuremberg, in the case of Ernst von Weizsäcker, former state secretary for foreign affairs. His deposition was published by journalist Margaret Boveri, under the title *Der Diplomat vor Gericht* (A Diplomat Before the Court of Justice), 1948; she sent Benn a copy, which became the source of this quotation. Benn resumed it in the last part of his radio-play, *The Voice Behind the Screen*, ET 1996, p. 51.

Page 50: **people will seek death but**...: Reference to The Revelation of John, more widely known as the Apocalypse, 9, 1-6.

Page 51: **celebrated: defiantly**...:The intraductible German original by Goethe reads as follows: 'Allen Gewalten/Zum Trutz sich erhalten,/Nimmer sich beugen,/Kräftig sich zeigen,/Rufet die Arme/Der Götter herbei. It is the second of a two-stanza poem that had been part of *Lila*, a 1777 musical play by Goethe, and which was taken out of context and first printed separately in the Weimar Theatre-Calendar for 1778. Since then it has been known by its first line 'Feiger Gedanken' (Faint-hearted thoughts).

Page 51: **or Dehmel**:...:Richard Dehmel (1863-1920), German poet, forerunner of Expressionism in literature, whose life and artistic activity was dominated by the conflict between sensuality and ascetic self-discipline. Benn's quotation from his work has not been identified.

Page 51: **or Hebbel: 'To the Striplings'**...:Christian Hebbel (1813-1863), poet and dramatist, interested in the life of the lower classes, and in social change as a source of new moral values. Originally included in the cycle *Vermischte Gedichte*, and published in his Collected Poems, vol. I, in 1857. It is a long poem that begins as follows: 'Trinkt des Weines dunkle Kraft,/ Die euch durch die Seele fließt/Und zu heil'ger Rechenschaft/Sie im Innersten erschließt!' (Drink the dark strength of the wine,/ which flows through your souls/ and to the saintly reckoning/ unlocks your inmost recesses!); and ends: 'Fort den Wein! Wer noch nicht flammt,/Ist nicht feines Kusses wert,/Und wer selbst vom Feuer stammt,/Steht schon lange glutverklärt./Euch geziemt nur eine Lust,/Nur ein Gang durch Sturm und Nacht,/Der aus eurer dunklen Brust/Einen Sternenhimmel macht.' (Off the wine! He who is not yet ablaze,/Is not worthy of fine kisses,/ And whoever emerges from the fire on his own/Stands a long time transfigured by the glow./Only a desire becomes you,/Only a passage through storm and night,/You who make a starry heaven/Out of your darkened breast.)

Page 53: **Shelley drowned**...:Percy Bysshe Shelley (1792-1822), English Romantic poet and controversial thinker.

Page 53: **Voltaire lived**...:Real name François-Marie Arouet (1694-1778), French writer and nonconformist thinker, settled on an estate in Switzerland in 1754.

Page 55: **but Fermi**...: Enrico Fermi (1901-1954), Italian-born American physicist, one of the main architects of the nuclear age, 1938 Nobel Prize winner, came to the US in 1938, and achieved the first controlled fission reaction at the University of Chicago in 1942.

BIOGRAPHICAL SUMMARY

1886-1896: Born on 2 May at the parsonage of Mansfeld, Westpriegnitz, second of the eight children of the Evangelical pastor Gustav Benn (1857–1939), and his French-Swiss wife Caroline, née Jequier (1858-1912); soon after his birth, the Benns moved to a larger parish at Sellin in Neumark, east of the Oder, where he spent his childhood.

1896-1911: Attends Friedrichs Gymnasium (Grammar School) at Frankfurt on the Oder; after graduation reads theology and philology at the University of Marburg for two years, then moves to Berlin where in 1905 is admitted on a scholarship to the Kaiser-Wilhelm Akademie, Berlin's famous school of military medicine; wins prize for his research on the aetiology of epilepsy at puberty; internship at the Charité Hospital in the German capital.

1912-1917: Successfully defends his MD dissertation on the frequency of diabetes melitus in the army; publication of a first cycle of poems, *Morgue und andere Gedichte* (Mortuary and Other Poems); friendship with poetess Else Lasker-Schüler; death of mother; military doctor; after less than a year quits the Army for health reasons; does work in pathology; publishes a new cycle of poems, *Söhne. Neue Gedichte* (Sons. New Poems); meets his future wife, the actress Edith Osterloh, whom he marries on 30 July 1914, after his career as ship doctor for Hapag is cut short by his physical unfitness for the job; WWI; is recalled by the Army very soon after the wedding; participates in the German campaign in Belgium; his daughter Nelle is born in 1915; first book of prose *Gehirne* (Brains) in 1916, and a new cycle of poems *Fleisch* (Flesh) is brought out a year later, when he is released from the Army, once again, for health reasons, and establishes his own practice for dermatology and venereal diseases in Berlin, which he closes only at the end of 1934.

1917-1936: Publishes *Das Moderne Ich* (The Modern I) in 1920; two years later his wife dies at Jena, following a surgical intervention, and publisher Erich Reiss brings out his first *Gesammelte Schriften* (Collected Writings) in Berlin; vain search for a better remunerated position as physician; goes on writing and publishing new cycles of poems; joins the PEN-club; new friendships with George Grosz, Oskar Loerke, Albert Flechtheim and Tilly Wedekind; *Gesammelte Gedichte* (Collected Poems) is published in 1927, followed a year later by *Gesammelte Prosa* (Collected Prose); in 1929, his ladyfriend, actress Lili Breda, commits suicide; writes the text for the oratorio *Das Unaufhörliche* (The Perpetual) with music by Paul Hindemith, performed in 1931 under the baton of Otto Klemperer; member of the literary section of the Prussian Academy of the Arts in 1932; unequal struggle with the dark forces of obscurantism intent on submerging German culture makes him seek refuge with the Army, which eventually accepts him and stands by him against the attacks of the SS that intensify after the publication of the volume of selected poems on the occasion of his fiftieth anniversary; forbidden not only to publish but also to write.

1937-1956: Transferred to military headquarters in Berlin; marries a second time; WWII; before September 1943, when his service is transferred to Landsberg-upon-the-Warthe, east of the Oder, about which he writes 'Barrack II - Room 66', one of the chapters of his panorama DOUBLE LIFE (1950), manages to have printed illegally his most recent poems in a private edition of five copies, under the title *Twenty-Two Poems*, 'Monologue' features among them; in 1945, as the Eastern Front collapses, flees back to Berlin and sends his wife to safety not far from Hamburg; she commits suicide when the Soviet Army replaces the Americans in the village of refuge; is forbidden to publish by the Allied Forces; in December 1946, marries Dr Ilse Kaul, a dentist, who moves her practice in his apartment; two years later, the Swiss publisher Arche Verlag brings out a selection of his underground poems, *Statische Gedichte* (Static Poems); then a Wiesbaden publisher steps in, and Benn is relaunched on his public literary career; in 1951 receives the Büchner Prize of the Darmstadt Academy; in 1953, awarded the Cross of the Order of Merit of the German Federal Republic; lectures, radio talks, essays about art and artists in the modern world; on 7 July 1956 dies of cancer of the spine and is buried in the American zone of Berlin.

SHORT BIBLIOGRAPHY

Benn, Gottfried. PRIMAL VISION: SELECTED WRITINGS, ed. E.B. Ashton. New York, 1960, 1971.

Benn, Gottfried. SELECTED POEMS, ed. F.W. Wodtke. Intro. and notes in English, poems in German. London, 1970.

Benn, Gottfried. PROSE, ESSAYS, POEMS, ed. Volkmar Sander. New York, 1987.

Benn, Gottfried. POEMS: 1937-1947. German and English. Tr. and Intro. Simona Draghici. Washington DC, 1991, 1997.

Benn, Gottfried.THE VOICE BEHIND THE SCREEN. Tr. and Intro. Simona Draghici. Washington DC, 1996.

Benn, Gottfried. DOUBLE LIFE. Ed., tr. and pref. Simona Draghici. Corvallis OR, 2002.

Benn, Gottfried. GOTTFRIED BENN IN TRANSITION. Ed. and Intro. Simona Draghici. Corvallis OR, 2003.

Benn, Gottfried. AUSGEWÄLTE BRIEFE, Postface Max Rychner. Wiesbaden, 1957, 1959.

Benn, Gottfried. BRIEFE AN F.W. OELZE: 1932-1956. Two volumes in three parts. Eds. Harald Steinhagen and Jürgen Schröder. Wiesbaden/Munich, 1977-1980.

Benn, Gottfried. BRIEFE AN TILLY WEDEKIND: 1930-1955. Ed. M.V. Schlüter. Stuttgart, 1986.

Benn, Gottfried. GESAMMELTE WERKE IN VIER BÄNDE. Ed. Dieter Wellershoff. Wiesbaden, 1958-1961.

Benn, Gottfried. GESAMMELTE WERKE IN DER FASSUNG DER ERST-DRUCKE. VIER BÄNDE. Ed. Bruno Hillebrand. Frankfurt am Main, 1984-1990.

Benn, Gottfried. SAMMTLICHE WERKE. Seven volumes. Eds. Gerhard Schuster and Holger Hof. Stuttgart, 1986-2002.

Adams, Marion. GOTTFRIED BENN'S CRITIQUE OF SUBSTANCE. Assen, 1969.

Alter, Reinhard. GOTTFRIED BENN: THE ARTIST AND POLITICS. Bern, 1976.

Dierick, A.P.. GOTTFRIED BENN AND HIS CRITICS. Columbia SC, 1992.

Eliot, T.S.. THREE VOICES OF POETRY. London, 1953.

Manyoni, Angelica. CONSISTENCY OF PHENOTYPE. Bern, 1983.

Ray, Susan. GOTTFRIED BENN'S POSTMODERNIST POETICS. New York, 2003.

Ritchie, James McPherson. GOTTFRIED BENN: THE UNRECONSTRUCTED EXPRESSIONIST. London, 1972.

Roche, M.W.. GOTTFRIED BENN'S STATIC POETRY. Chapel Hill NC, 1991.

Travers, Martin. CRITICS OF MODERNITY. New York, 2001.

About the Editor

SIMONA DRAGHICI is a European–American social scientist who among other things holds a PhD degree in sociology from the University of Texas at Austin. Her interests in the comparative study of social institutions have led her more recently to the analysis of the recurrent phenomenon of civilizational decline.